Visito
Ge
Rhine

D0443992

RHINE AND
MOSEL

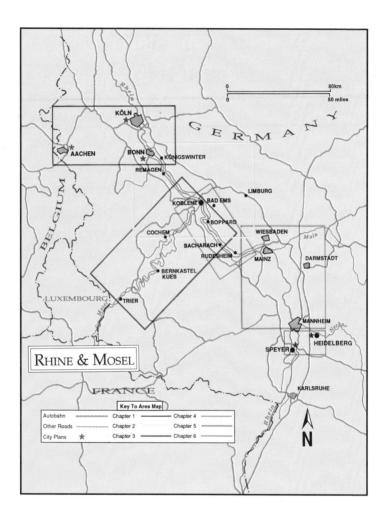

RHINE & MOSEL

VISITOR'S GUIDE
GERMANY:
RHINE & MOSEL

JOHN MARSHALL

MPC

HUNTER

Published by:
Moorland Publishing Co Ltd,
Moor Farm Road West,
Ashbourne,
Derbyshire DE6 1HD
England

ISBN 0 86190 188 6

Published in the USA by:
Hunter Publishing Inc,
300 Raritan Center Parkway,
CN 94, Edison, NJ 08818

ISBN 1 55650 535 3 (USA)

British Library Cataloguing in
Publication Data:
A catalogue record for this book is
available from the British Library.

Colour origination by:
P. & W. Graphics Pte Ltd, Singapore

Printed in Great Britain by
Bath Press Colourbooks, Glasgow

Cover photograph: Bad Ems
(*Bad Ems Verkehrsdirektion*)

Illustrations have been supplied as
follows: Asbach Distillery page
115(top); Köln-Düsseldorfer
German Rhine Line pages 10, 18;
J. Marshall pages 44, 46, 62
(lower), 63, 66, 74, 78, 87 (top), 99,
102, 103, 107, 111, 147, 152; MPC
Picture Collection pages 34, 35, 39,
50, 60, 62 (top), 70-1, 75, 87 (lower),
91, 116 (lower), 127; and the tourist
information offices of: Köln page
19; Idar-Oberstein page 79; Mainz
page 134; Rheinhessen (Schultz/
Kilian) page 114, (Europress) page
131 (top), (Wibo-Werburg) page
131 (lower); Trier page 83

MPC Production Team:
Editorial and Design: John Robey
Cartography: Alastair Morrison
Typesetting: Christine Haines and
Kirsty Haines

About the Author:
John Marshall, a former headmas-
ter, is an inveterate student of
languages and civilizations, ancient
and modern, and has travelled
widely in Europe and the Mediterranean. He has made numerous
visits to Germany over a period of
many years, especially in the Rhine
and Mosel area. He is the author of
Visitor's Guide to Switzerland and
has contributed to *Off The Beaten
Track: Switzerland*. He lives in
Scotland.

CONTENTS

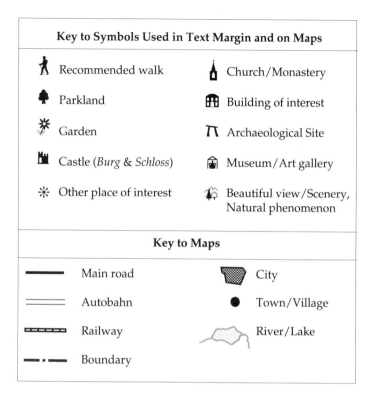

Key to Symbols Used in Text Margin and on Maps

🚶 Recommended walk

🌳 Parkland

🌼 Garden

🏰 Castle (*Burg* & *Schloss*)

❋ Other place of interest

⛪ Church/Monastery

🏛 Building of interest

П Archaeological Site

🖼 Museum/Art gallery

🌲 Beautiful view/Scenery, Natural phenomenon

Key to Maps

▬▬▬ Main road

═══ Autobahn

▬▭▭▬ Railway

▬ · ▬ Boundary

🗑 City

⚫ Town/Village

〰 River/Lake

How To Use This Guide

This MPC Visitor's Guide has been designed to be as easy to use as possible. Each chapter covers a region or itinerary in a natural progression which gives all the background information to help you enjoy your visit. MPC's distinctive margin symbols, the important places printed in bold, and a comprehensive index enable the reader to find the most interesting places to visit with ease. At the end of each chapter an Additional Information section gives specific details such as addresses and opening times, making this guide a complete sightseeing companion. At the back of the guide the Fact File, arranged in alphabetical order, gives practical information and useful tips to help you plan your holiday — before you go and while you are there. The maps of each region show the main towns, villages, roads and places of interest, but are not designed as route maps and motorists should always use a good recommended road atlas.

INTRODUCTION

'Rhine' and 'Romantic'. Both in English and in German the couplet trips off the tongue so readily, conjuring up pictures of castles on crags, steep terraced slopes of vineyards facing the sun, riverside villages and towns of fascinating medieval aspect and bright with flowers, vessels gliding serenely downstream or surging upstream with a creaming bow-wave. It is an interesting thought that the picturesque character of this region of Germany and the fascination it holds for visitors derive from one or two hard facts of geography — and the influence they exerted on human history.

The main fact is the immense massif of hard rock which Germans call the Rheinisches Schiefergebirge (Rhenish Schist Uplands) that blocks off northern from southern Germany. When the earth was young the river Rhine, flowing northward from the Alps to the North Sea, had to find a line of least resistance through the massive plateau of slate. And tributaries such as the Mosel from the south-west and the Lahn from the east contributed to a process that carved up the plateau into four land-masses of surprising symmetry: the high rolling upland regions of great natural beauty that form the Eifel and Hunsrück west of the Rhine, the Westerwald and Taunus to its east.

The Rhine valley itself inevitably became not only man's principal avenue between Northern and Southern Germany, but also the main northern section of the trade route for exotic goods and equally of crafts and skills between southern Europe and the Mediterranean lands on the one hand and Northern Europe on the other. It was the highway which linked two European regions which had the most unsettled, turbulent and complex history of all in early, medieval and even comparatively modern times: Germany and Italy.

Just to the south of the Rhine gorge, where this precipitous canyon through the slate uplands appears in its most dramatic form, the

Rhine flows peacefully through the level and fertile landscapes of the Rhine Plain. To the east here, edging the valleys of the rivers Main and Neckar, lie open approaches to fertile land which simply beckoned nomadic or raiding tribes from the east. This was the geographical lay-out that set the scene for the many turbulent tribal migrations that afflicted Europe in general, but above all the Rhinelands, in the early centuries of the Christian era.

Archaeological evidence reveals that before these migrations many of today's Rhineland towns and cities had already existed as Celtic hill forts. After the Romans occupied Gaul and found the Germanic tribes to the east of the Rhine a hornet's nest of trouble they ultimately became persuaded to hold the Rhine as an eastern frontier and they converted many Celtic hill-forts to Roman strong-points. However, soon learning that a river is not so effective a barrier as it seems, they advanced their frontier zone of defence in depth many kilometres east of the river. It is a frequent source of surprise to first-time visitors to Rhineland towns — and perhaps even more so to the Mosel area — to discover the extent of surviving Roman remains. This provides evidence of how thorough was the Romanisation of the land west of the Rhine. Eventually the pressure from Germanic tribes forced the Romans back to the Rhine itself and ultimately in the fifth century to withdraw altogether.

The German history of the 'dark ages' and the medieval period is too complex for this brief introduction. Yet one or two salient points should be mentioned to help an understanding of Rhineland landscapes and institutions. At the turn of the ninth century a king of the Frankish tribe of Germans whose name is most readily recognised in its French form, Charlemagne, forged a unitary realm of diverse nations and tongues in Western Europe which he clearly conceived as a Germanic and Christian version of the defunct Roman Empire in the west. It was only after his death that the West Franks came to regard themselves as of French nationality and the East Franks of German, as in the hands of his successors the realm became fragmented. In the medieval period when French and English kings were gradually bringing to heel the great territorial magnates and making their realms effective kingdoms, the German lands remained fragmented. For although the German lands had an Emperor his selection was made by an electoral council as there was distrust of a hereditary system. The electoral system often led to candidates being chosen who would be no great threat to the independence of the princes who elected them. Inevitably at times such a choice was so mediocre as to leave the realm vulnerable to the external pressures from intruders that still plagued it from the east and the north. That

Some Words Seen on Signposts or Public Notices

Abfahrt	departure	*Hauptbahnhof*	main railway station
Altstadt	old town		
Ankunft	arrival	*Hauptpost*	main post office
Anlegestelle	mooring place, pier	*Kirche*	church
		Mühle	mill
Aufzug	lift, elevator	*Pfad*	path
Ausgang	exit	*Platz*	square
Bad	spa town	*Rathaus*	town hall
Bahnhof	railway station	*Saal*	hall, large room
Berg	mountain, hill	*Stadt*	city/town
Brücke	bridge	*Tal*	valley
Brunnen	spring, fountain	*Turm*	tower
Dom	cathedral	*Ufer*	shore, riverbank
Dorf	village		
Einbahnstrasse	one-way street	*Verboten*	prohibited
Eingang	entrance	*Verbotener Eingang*	keep out!
Fähre	ferry		
Fussgänger	pedestrians	*Verkehr*	traffic/tourism
Gasse	narrow street, lane	*Vorsicht*	watch out!, beware!
Gefahr	danger	*Weg*	path
Haltestelle	stopping place (bus, etc)	*Zimmer*	(bed) room
		Zimmer Frei	room(s) to let

is but one element in a situation that kept Germany a nation divided into independent realms where dukes, electoral princes, counts and lesser noblemen ruled — and co-operated only when desperate situations drove them to it — at times belatedly.

Thus the numerous castles of the Rhineland regions are not so much as a sign of regional strength and unity to face external aggression but of internal divisions. Yet external hostilities were recurrent, including embroilments in Italy. For although the concept of a Holy Roman Empire of the Germans implied co-operation between Emperor and Pope as temporal and spiritual leaders respectively, the contrary was at times the case — indeed, during the eleventh century to a highly damaging extent.

A fragmented and disunited Germany was ill-equipped to stand up to what became the powerfully centralised kingdom of France with ambitions to extend its eastern frontier to the Rhine. Everywhere in the Rhineland areas the visitor will see and hear evidence

The Rhine has always been an important highway — a river-cruise ship and commercial boats pass the Pfalz at Kaub, built to collect tolls from the river traffic

of the impact of the armies of Louis XIV in the late seventeenth-century war usually described as the War over the Palatinate Succession. And in many places too one learns of fairly sweeping changes that were brought to the region by Napoleon's invasion and also, later, by the peace which followed, bringing most of the Rhineland under the rule of the Prussian Kingdom.

Since World War II West Germany has been a Federal Republic, the parts of which are called *Länder*, literally 'lands' but difficult to translate adequately into any one-word English equivalent. The areas covered by this book lie largely in the federal state of Rheinland-Pfalz (Rhineland-Palatinate), with its administrative capital and parliament in the historic city of Mainz. But an important northern section which includes the great city of Köln, the one-time capital of Charlemagne's empire, Aachen, and the post-war federal capital, Bonn, lies in Nordrhein-Westfalen (North Rhine and Westphalia). An important stretch of the east bank of the Rhine gorge, from Kaub southward and continuing into the noble winelands of the Rheingau, fall into the state of Hessen (capital Wiesbaden). Finally, Heidelberg, one-time capital of the Palatinate, now lies within the boundaries of Baden-Württemberg.

At numerous places in the Rhenish Schist Uplands—especially on the fringes — there are natural springs that produce mineral water, sometimes quite warm. Because of this there are quite a number of spas in the hill country and on the edges of the Schist Mountain districts: the Eifel, Hunsrück, Taunus and Westerwald. The English word 'spa' is derived from the health resort of Spa, on the fringe of the Eifel, on the Belgian side, about 40km (25 miles) from Aachen. The German word for a spa however is *Bad* — which also means a 'bath'. Aachen is sometimes called Bad Aachen, for instance.

Since even before the Roman era the beneficial effects of fresh air, water, restful surroundings, pleasant scenery and climate were recognised. Spa towns try to provide their visitors with all these as well as social, cultural and musical recreation. For visitors with specific health problems there are clinics and doctors to advise on the best therapies which usually include the drinking of mineral waters from the local sources, swimming or water exercises, perhaps massage and hot mud baths to ease painful conditions, and all prescribed and supervised by qualified persons. Spa treatments are very popular in Germany as a refreshing and restorative kind of holiday; but for certain health problems people can get assistance towards the cost of spa residence from the German system of private medical insurance.

1
KÖLN, AACHEN AND BONN

Köln (Cologne)

Although Cologne is a city of about one million inhabitants, the vitality and variety of its institutions and activities give it great appeal to all kinds of visitors.

The German form of the city's name is **Köln**, although ironically its English form sounds closer to its original Roman name of *Colonia Agrippensis*. The word *colonia* means that it was a community with the proper legal constitution, institutions and rights of a Roman city — but whose founding citizens were veteran soldiers of the Roman army. Placed at a strategic situation usually near a frontier, it would serve both as an example of Roman civilisation and as a source of capable citizens with an army background in times of emergency on the frontier. Köln came into existence, in short, because of its key position on the Rhine, where military and trade routes from south, west, north and east met.

That position on the Rhine guaranteed the city an important role from Roman times, right through the Middle Ages, up to today, as a pulsating centre of trade and commerce. Its modern trade fairs, for which it is known throughout the world, are the inheritors of the tradition of the great annual markets of the Middle Ages.

Despite the size of the modern city, its heart is still beside and alongside the river. The best way to get to know the heart of a city is on foot. Köln is one of those fortunate cities where you can get a good sample of its life and atmosphere from a short walk through its heart. But first, it is well worthwhile taking a look at its setting by viewing its famous Rhine-front panorama as seen from the east bank.

The historic city lies, of course, on the west bank. And its heart is easily found. The unmistakeable silhouette of the twin spires of the cathedral can be seen from afar and lead to the city's heart. Very near to the cathedral is the main station, and the architect had the imagination and flair to design the tall wall that looks over from the station to the cathedral to be made of glass.

The nearby Hohenzollernbrücke which crosses the Rhine to the district of Deutz (where the famous Trade Fair centre is sited), carries both the railway and pedestrians, with easy access for the latter from the cathedral precincts or the western riverfront. Use it to reach the east bank where there is an elevated viewpoint beside the bridge. Looking across, you can pick out prominent points in the old town, from right to left from the bridge: the cathedral; beside it the modern complex of the Wallraf Richartz-Museum together with the Philharmonie concert hall; the next tall Romanesque tower is of the Gross St Martin Kirche (High Church of St Martin); further back and further left the next tower is the Rathausturm; thereafter near the waterfront the pointed gables and colourful façades of the old-world narrow houses of the Martinsviertel (St Martin Quarter, a more specific name for the old town). Along the water-front in the foreground are the landing stages for the white excursion ships of the Köln-Düsseldorfer German Rhine Line.

On recrossing the Hohenzollernbrücke is an area of recent development lying between river front, cathedral and the **Altstadt**. The obviously modern building complex here is the home of the **Wallraf-Richartz and Ludwig Museums** of European painting; below the museums is the city's giant new Philharmonie concert hall, accommodating 2,000 people. Towards the cathedral's east end on the left is the square building of the **Römisch-Germanisches Museum**. This building was erected over the remarkable Roman Dionysos Mosaic, which was found during World War II when an air-raid shelter was being built. It covers an area of 70sq metres (756sq ft). The museum has an interesting collection of artefacts illustrating everyday life in Roman Köln; but it also deals beyond the Roman era to the days of the Emperor Charlemagne.

The **cathedral** itself, landmark and emblem of the city, shows an impressive harmony of high Gothic style, despite the fact that, altough commenced in 1248AD — the most ambitious design of its era, and influenced by Chartres and Amiens — it was not completed until 1842. When 90 per cent of Köln old town lay in ruins after World War II, the cathedral though seriously damaged still stood. The greatest of its many treasures are the massive thirteenth-century Reliquary of the Three Kings (or Magi) above the high altar and — in the ambulatory behind the altar — the fifteenth-century triptych painting *Adoration of the Kings*. The cathedral treasury contains precious ecclesiastical goldsmith work, vestments and utensils.

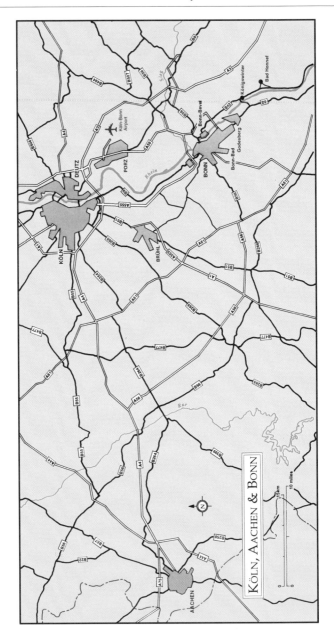

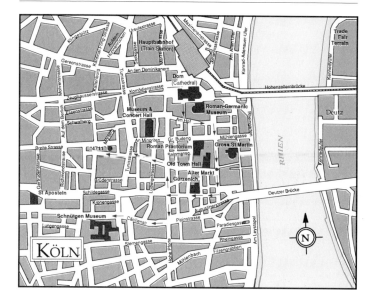

A WALK THROUGH THE OLD TOWN

Almost facing the main portal of the cathedral, slightly to the right is the tourist information office, which has available a great variety of tourist brochures and leaflets on all aspects of the city and surroundings. To its left, directly facing the cathedral, is the starting point for city sightseeing tours by bus.

The following short walk through the old town is mostly in pedestrian precinct areas. Until very recently the old town had been cut off from the nearby Rhine by the continuous stream of vehicular traffic along a main Rhine-bank roadway. That traffic has now been channelled into a six-lane tunnel and over it a new Rhine garden that is linked with the alleyways of the old town has been laid. The fringe of this area is enhanced by the colourful umbrellas and awnings of the small cafés and stalls that give the place an inviting atmosphere, and the whole forms a splendid promenade area.

Leaving the cathedral and passing on the left the front of the Roman-Germanic Museum, cross straight over into the street called Unter Goldschmied, and head into the precincts of the **Old Town Hall**, lying on your left, until a little street named Kleine Budengasse is reached on the left. There you can visit, in the basement area of the New City Hall complex, the remains of the *Praetorium*, one-time headquarters of the Roman provincial governor. From the Kleine

Budengasse, turn right into Bürgerstrasse to reach the front of the late Gothic town hall and admire the elegant Renaissance porch built out in front of the handsome chamber. This is associated with the powerful medieval Hanseatic League of northern trading cities, of which Köln was one. Opposite the town hall porch is the excavated site of part of the Great Hall of the Roman palace.

Beside the impressive tower of the town hall there is a flight of steps leading down to the **Alter Markt**, now also part of the traffic-free zone. Over the Alter Markt towards the riverside can be seen the lofty Romanesque tower of the **Gross St Martin Kirche** which has given its name to this quarter of the old town — and is a prominent feature of the river front panorama seen from the opposite bank. It repays a visit, being one of a remarkable ring of twelve Romanesque churches built in Köln from the tenth to mid-thirteenth centuries, during a period of expanding trade and wealth that followed the reign of Charlemagne that was the zenith of Köln's prosperity.

But the Alter Markt also illustrates the reputation of Köln's old town for a nineteenth-century atmosphere of joviality and conviviality in romantic old-world nooks and crannies. There are several traditional ale houses and eating places in and around the Alter Markt, such as the Gaffelhaus traditional restaurant at Alter Markt 20-22. At Papa Joe's Biersalon, Alter Markt 50-52, traditional New Orleans jazz is played.

Although Rhine most appropriately rhymes with wine (both in German and English) and Köln lies only a short distance from the Rhenish winelands and so has its wine bars, the city is really famed for its own special brew of beer called *kölsch*. The dialect adjective *kölsch* means belonging to Köln; but when the word is used on its own, as a noun, it means the local beer of very individual character. And the serving of *kölsch* in a traditional ale house is a cult that has its own ceremonies, customs and cheerful atmosphere. A typical one can be found by heading down the Alter Markt (keeping the riverbank garden area on the left) into the Heumarkt (Haymarket) where at No 60 is the Altstadt-Paffgen (Paffgen being the name of one of the typical family-owned small breweries) where you may sample *kölsch*; you can lunch here too from a choice of inexpensive Rhineland specialities.

From the Heumarkt the Gürzenichstrasse leads away from the river, and soon intersects the Unter Goldschmied. Turn right into this again to reach the handsome Gothic banqueting and festival hall called the **Gürzenich**, built in 1437-44, rebuilt after World War II destruction, and used today for official receptions, concerts and carnival events. Leaving it, take the Obenmarspforte (heading again away from the river) to reach its intersection with the pedestrian precinct stretch of the Hohe-strasse. Turn right into this, which is a distinguished and elegant traffic-free shopping street, full of colour and vitality. It leads back to the cathedral precinct.

Before walking back up the Hohe-strasse, if you have time there are two interesting detours possible. Instead of turning left into Hohe-strasse continue straight on. Obenmarspforte continues into Brückengasse and, having crossed the wide Tunis-strasse, then becomes Glockengasse. Where Glockengasse begins, at the Offenbachplatz, there is a large building in Renaissance style which bears what is probably the most famous house number in the world, having become a trade mark: 4711. House numbers were given to all ✳ buildings here when the Rhineland was taken over by French armies in 1794. It so happened that just a few years previously the apothecary who lived there had produced for the first time '*Echt Kölnisch Wasser*' — or as the world has come to know it *Eau de Cologne*. The building, now a perfume exhibition centre, has a clock which chimes each hour from 9am to 9pm while painted figures — a metre high — perform a parade. So try to arrive there shortly before the hour is due to strike.

The other optional extension to the walk is to continue down towards the south end of Hohe-strasse, ie in the opposite direction from the cathedral, to where it intersects with Caecilienstrasse. There turn right. Shortly, on the left, is the former Church of St Cecilia which now houses, very appropriately and spaciously in the eight-centuries old Romanesque basilica, the unique **Schnütgen-Museum** ⌂ **of Medieval Church Art**.

People in Köln have a saying that their city does not merely have four seasons of year but five, the fifth one being Carnival Time. *Fastelovend* or Carnival is the traditional time for people to dress up and enjoy themselves (originally to celebrate the passing of winter). Between New Year's Eve and the start of Lent more than 300 carnival balls take place. The season comes to a climax on *Weiberfastnacht* (Women's Carnival) on the Thursday before Lent begins, when a time of merry-making in the streets is officially proclaimed at the Alter Markt. The following days are also marked with processions, the main one being on Rosenmontag (Rose Monday), the Monday preceding Ash Wednesday. For anyone planning a winter holiday in Germany, this is a time to consider. The tourist office publishes an annual timetable of Carnival events, available from the previous November onwards.

To gain a more comprehensive impression of the city there is much to be said for taking a sightseeing bus tour from the cathedral portals.

This is a convenient way of seeing the famed and unique ring of lovely churches of the Romanesque period.

A considerable range of river excursions is offered by various boat operators, from trips of an hour or two that cover the city's river banks on both sides to lengthy day tours which visit classic Rhine resorts and beauty spots upstream. There are even holiday cruises of several days, such as those run by the Köln-Dusseldorfer German Rhine Line. Information on these can be obtained from the tourist office, and tickets at the jetties on the (west) embankment between the Hohenzollern and Deutzer bridges.

Köln cathedral from the Rhine, with the old town on the left

Köln is well off for recreational parks, with the Zoological Gardens and Aquarium on the northern fringe of the city and conveniently reached by tram routes 5, 15, 16 and 18. Next to the zoo are the Botanical Gardens. A trip to the zoo area can be extended in summertime by taking the aerial cableway that takes you in gondola cars 930m (3,051ft) across the Rhine (getting a marvellous view of Köln and the cathedral on the way) to the extensive and varied Rhine Park on the east bank where there is dancing, popular summer shows, children's playgrounds, miniature railway, etc.

EXCURSIONS FROM KÖLN

Within no more than an hour's drive of Köln are many interesting excursions, such as the fringe of the ruggedly romantic Eifel Hills to

Christmas shopping at 4711 Köln, the trade mark of Eau de Cologne

the south-west, or the Siebengebirge (Seven Mountains) on the far bank of the Rhine to the south-east (see Chapter 2).

Just under 15km (9 miles) south of Köln is the town of **Brühl**, reached on road B51 through Köln's outer green belt. In Brühl is Schloss Augustusburg (often known simply as Schloss Brühl) a show-piece baroque residential palace, built in rococo style in 1725 by world-famous architects and artists as a summer residence for the Archbishop of Cologne. It has one of the most magnificent staircases of that period with gorgeous stucco work and elegantly decorative wrought-iron balustrades. To match the splendid interior are equally magnificent furnishings — priceless tapestries and Delft wall tiling; in keeping with the castle is the delightful formal baroque garden setting that takes in on its verge the charming Falkenlust Hunting Lodge. The palace is used today by the German Government for official state receptions and functions, but at other times is open to the public for visits. Continuing by road for a short distance beyond Brühl one arrives at **Phantasialand**, 30,000sq metres of amusement and adventure park for children (of all ages) — Germany's version of EuroDisney — with its Pirate Ship, Wild West Town, circus, many water sports and dolphin shows and much else.

Instead of returning to Köln from Phantasialand one can continue on the same road to Bonn (see later section of this chapter).

Aachen

Although the city of Aachen does not lie on the Rhine it belongs to the Rhineland and for a lengthy era played a key role in the shaping of Rhineland history. It was the residence of Charlemagne when both Rhine banks were united into a single realm, and it was the place where German kings were crowned. When Napoleon later incorporated into France the lands up to the west bank of the Rhine, the city was given the name Aix-la-Chapelle, which still crops up in history books.

Aachen, situated close to where three countries meet, is one of those places where the motorist has to be on the alert for alternative versions of the name. The French form Aix-la-Chapelle has already been mentioned. The Dutch form of the name, Aken, occurs not only on signposts in Holland, but also in Flemish-speaking areas of Belgium. Between Aachen and the Channel coast, further west, lies the great Belgian city of Liege. On the motorways nowadays different-looking place names suddenly appear as you pass from one language zone to another; signposts for Liege appear as Luik in Dutch/Flemish areas and as Lüttich in German!

The direct route from Köln to Aachen by road is by the very busy

Autobahn A4. But there is a good railway service (DB Timetable 440) which does the 40km (25 miles) in about 45 minutes. The best starting point for a walk in the historical core of the city is the Markt; from the railway station this can be reached by way of Bahnhofplatz, Bahnhofstrasse, turn left into Theater-strasse at the end of which lies the Grabenring (a circle of streets on the site of former defence walls). The Markt lies at the centre of this circle; approach by Hartmann-strasse and then the pedestrian precincts of the courtyards of the cathedral and town hall.

The Markt is spacious enough for one to stand back and admire the decorated Gothic style of the **town hall** which was built on the foundations of Charlemagne's early ninth-century palace. The citizens of Aachen started to build their town hall in the early fourteenth century. One of its main features was to provide a banqueting hall for royal coronations. So its impressive Krönungs-saal (Coronation Hall), having survived various reconstructions and restorations, well repays a visit. Externally, the north façade overlooking the market place is adorned with the statues of fifty German sovereigns — thirty-one of whom were crowned here. The small unusual-looking tower in front of the east face of the building is an important architectural remain of Carolingian date, part of the imperial living quarters. In the interior of the building is a collection of Crown Jewels associated with great ceremonial occasions.

Turning right on leaving the town hall take the most frequented of the city's pedestrian precincts, the Krämer-strasse to the **cathedral**, one of Europe's most eminent architectural monuments. At the core of the building is the octagonal rotunda in Byzantine style erected by Charlemagne about the year 800 as a royal palace chapel. After Charlemagne was beatified in 1165 the then Emperor Frederick Barbarossa commissioned a reliquary to be made to hold the remains of the dead Charlemagne which is considered to be one of the great achievements of Rhenish goldsmiths' art of the High Middle Ages. Of approximately the same date is Barbarossa's other munificent gift, the stupendously great candelabrum in the rotunda. Two of the cathedral's other unique possessions are Charlemagne's late eighth-century white marble throne, striking in its simplicity, and the copper-gilt pulpit that dates from the start of the twelfth century. In later Middle Ages a number of side chapels were erected around the original octagon and choir. Nor should the visitor to the cathedral fail to visit the Domschatz (Cathedral Treasury); the collections of ecclesiastical robes, reliquaries, monstrances and biblical codices that have accumulated in more than a thousand years make Aachen's treasures the most priceless this side of the Alps.

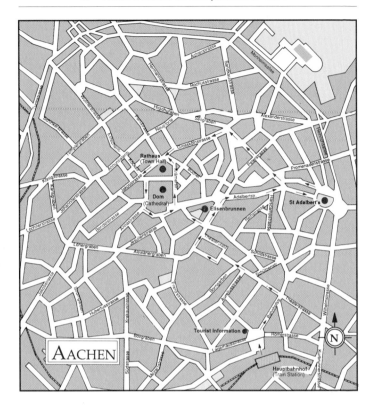

Little wonder then that Aachen has drawn flocks of pilgrims throughout the centuries. Another steady stream of visitors came over the centuries for the thermal springs, which attracted the Romans to this corner of their Gallic provinces in the first place. Aachen has been a spa since Roman times. On leaving the cathedral precinct again by Hartmannstrasse you find on the left, as the Ring is reached again, the substantial emblem of Aachen's status as a spa — the ornamental fountain known as the Elisenbrunnen. This building, lying beyond a small garden-park, takes the form of a Rotunda with a public drinking fountain, where the thermal spa water can be sampled. (The main spa centres with thermal baths, gardens, clinics, sanitoria and spa-hotels specialising in therapeutic services lie in two areas outside the Ring, one to the north, the Monheimsallee district, the other to the south, beyond the main railway station, the Burtscheid spa-district.)

From the Elisen fountain walk diagonally to the left, across the Ring avenue (this section being called Friedrich-Wilhelm Platz) to a wide traffic-free street, Adalbert-strasse. You can then return, recrossing the Ring into further pedestrian zone streets, Holz-graben and adjacent Dahmen-graben with their boutiques and galleries, and then by Grossköln-strasse back to the Markt where the walk started.

As in most cities that cater for all-year-round spa guests, Aachen has a good provision of the arts, music, theatre and most kinds of entertainment and recreation. A new style of contemporary art museum, for instance, the Ludwig Forum for International Art, was opened in 1991.

On the first weekend of September every year the European Market for Art and Crafts is held. About 400 craftsmen from all over Europe set up their exhibits in the city-centre precincts bringing colour and bustle to the neighbourhood of the cathedral and town hall: puppet modellers, glass etchers, silk painters, gold and silver-smiths, glass blowers — and, of course, musicians and singers join in the scene.

Another annual event in the neighbourhood is an international horse jumping tournament. This brings champion riders and horse lovers to the Soers valley (which lies just to the north of the city) from all over the world. Horse riding is in any case a local activity; there is a network of some 50km (31 miles) of bridle paths in the Forest of Aachen.

Bonn

Visitors using public transport will probably return from Aachen to Köln before passing on to Bonn. Those using private transport may be tempted to travel south from Aachen, skirting the Belgian frontier, into the Eifel, a route described in Chapter 3. A compromise for motorists wishing to avoid using the *Autobahn* for their return from Aachen would be to use regional road B264 via Eschweiler to Düren, there turning right onto road B56 which passes by way of Zülpich and Euskirchen to enter Bonn from the west (a total of 110km, 68 miles). Euskirchen, a town manufacturing woollens, has an interest-ing medieval town hall and church.

Before World War II (in which its historic town centre was sub-stantially destroyed and then virtually reconstructed in the post-war era) Bonn was a sedate small provincial university town on an attractive site on the river bank facing, across the water, the heights of the Siebengebirge (Seven Mountains). In 1949 it was made the seat of the Federal Government, and since then it has virtually doubled its population.

As is the case with so many Rhineland towns having a good site, Bonn had a Roman era as a full-strength legionary post, *Castra Bonnensia*. It was the residence of the Prince-Bishops of Cologne for some five centuries, and was occupied along with the rest of the Rhineland by Napoleonic armies. After Napoleon's defeat it was incorporated in Prussia in 1815, shortly thereafter acquiring its university.

The town centre is fairly easy to come to terms with, as an extensive pedestrian precinct lies inside a city traffic ring with parking lots at reasonable intervals. The precinct is best entered from the main railway station. From the post office at the main station Post-strasse leads to Münsterplatz where the main post office lies on the left facing the Beethoven Monument. Beethoven was born in Bonn in 1770. His birthplace honours his name with pride and his memorial is in front of the **Münster**, a basilica in Romanesque style, mostly of twelfth- and thirteenth-century origin. Its special features are the twelfth-century cloisters and a graceful tower. Leave the Münsterplatz by Remigius-strasse east of the minster, and turn right into Fürstenstrasse to reach Am Hof, a one-way street that is part of the traffic ring. On the opposite side of Am Hof are the main buildings of the Friedrich-Wilhelms-Universität, the university of Bonn, which occupy what was once the residential palace of the Prince-Electors of Cologne. By continuing north (left) in Am Hof you reach, on the left, the triangle-shaped Markt. On the nearest corner stands the eighteenth-century town hall, where an annex entered from Rathausgasse houses Bonn's art collection. The name Remigius given to the street near the Minster is explained by the existence of the fifteenth-century church of St Remigius which stands just north of the town hall but is reached by the Brüdergasse.

Bonn-gasse goes off from the western corner of the Markt and near its end, on the right hand, is house No 20 in which Beethoven was born. Looking much as it did in Beethoven's day, No 20 is now a museum holding many valuable exhibits including hand-written examples and early prints of important works, the composer's last grand piano and his string instruments. Bonn-gasse leads into the Bertha-von-Suttner-Platz (on right). By following its continuation into the avenue named Berliner Freiheit (Freedom for Berlin) you reach, appropriately, the Kennedybrücke (432m, 1,417ft long) which crosses the Rhine to Bonn's east-bank suburb, Beuel. Just upstream from the bridge is one of Bonn's river vessel landing stages, Alter Zoll (Old Toll). It is so called because of the monument close by upstream at the edge of the Stadtgarten marking where once stood the river traffic control tower at which tolls were exacted from passing ships.

Between the bridge and Alter Zoll along the Brassert-Ufer (*Ufer* means a shore or river bank) is the 900-seat opera house. (In the other direction from the bridge, downstream, the river bank avenue leads to the huge Beethovenhalle — where the largest hall seats 1,600 people — catering for concerts, congresses, exhibitions and the triennial Beethoven Festival.)

From the corner at the Alter Zoll monument take the street running from the river bank, Konviktstrasse, to where it crosses Adenauer-allee. At the junction is the Koblenzer Tor, the **Koblenz Gate**, built in the mid-eighteenth century in the form of a triumphal arch. From here the Adenauer-allee runs south to the entirely new area of Bonn, which had to be built to enable a fairly modest provincial town accommodate the administration of the Federal Republic and the residences of its prominent figures.

In the garden park called the Hofgarten, on the right, is the **Akademischer Kunstmuseum** (Academic Museum of Fine Art), while on the left is the university library. About $1^1/_2$km (1 mile) on, the Adenauer-allee (road B9) is joined from the west by Reuter-strasse which is a continuation in the city of national road A565. The junction called Bundeskanzlerplatz (Federal Chancellor Square), is the centre of the Government quarter. Opposite it stands the modern building of the Federal Chancellery. The parkland adjacent to the north holds the official residence of the Federal President (the Villa Hammerschmidt) and the Palais Schaumburg which for some years was the Chancellor's official home and office, later used for his official functions.

Nearer the river are the starker modern buildings of the Federal German Parliament, Upper House and Lower House. In the district to the west of these proliferate other official buildings and offices. There is a ship landing stage, Bundeshaus, on the riverfront. Further upstream, still on the riverfront, is the extensive city recreational park Rheinaue with views across the river to the Siebengebirge. The park and the river are crossed by the Konrad-Adenauer-Brücke which carries motorway A562 over to join the east bank motorway.

Before leaving the confines of Bonn proper, however, it is worth while, especially if using private transport, to go back to the Bundeskanzlerplatz road junction and take Reuter-strasse to the left, heading west. At the point where Reuterstrasse merges into the dual-carriageway A565, turn off right into the slip road for the **Botanical Gardens** and the **Schloss Poppelsdorf**, built in the early eighteenth century for the Prince Elector and now housing a Museum of Mineralogy. From there a return to the Hauptbahnhof can be made by taking the Meckenheimer Allee north. Before reaching the station

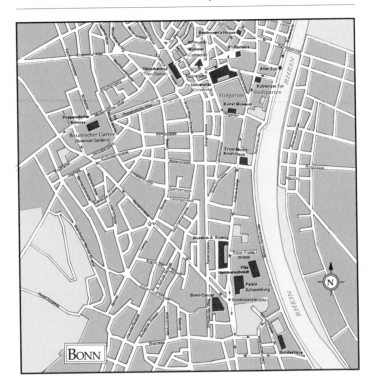

turn off into Colmant-strasse to visit the modern **Rhineland Museum** which portrays the history of the Rhineland from primeval times to modern.

Alternatively, from Schloss Poppelsdorf take the Meckenheimer Allee in the opposite direction, south, continuing by Clemens-August-strasse and Trierer-strasse to the Kreuzberg hill (125m, 410ft) where there is a *Wallfahrts-kirche* (pilgrimage church) of the early seventeenth century.

EXCURSIONS FROM BONN

Bad Godesberg, a spa resort 7km (4 miles) upstream from Bonn has in the post-war era been made an integral part of the city, and is readily reached by rail or by road B9. To an older generation it had the dubious fame of being in 1938 the scene of the meeting between Adolf Hitler and Neville Chamberlain, British prime minister, during the international crisis over the fate of Czechoslovakia. Today its amenities have made it a favourite commuter area for Federal Government senior officials employed in Bonn; a great number of foreign embassies are also sited here in the agreeable garden surroundings of a spa that dates back to Roman times.

Its extensive Stadtpark is famous even in a region of parks and gardens. It is reached by following the Poststrasse east from the railway station. In it is sited the Trinkpavillon where the mineral water from the Kurfürstenquelle, or Prince Elector's Spring, can be enjoyed. The Stadthalle, a venue for congresses, concerts and great occasions, is also in the park; during the summer season on Saturdays and Sundays regular 'Spa Concerts' take place on the terrace. In short, an enjoyable half-day or day can be spent in the Stadtpark and in the neighbouring Redoutenpark across the Kurfürstenallee. This was named after the Redoute, a rococo ballroom built for one of the Electors at the end of the eighteenth century, now used for concerts and receptions. In this park are also large thermal spa establishments with sophisticated equipment for treatments.

From the Redoutenpark or Stadtpark (west end) Schwertbergerstrasse and then Winterstrasse leads to the avenue Auf dem Godesberg on the right, and so ascend to Schloss Godesburg. The castle was built around 1210, besieged and blown up in 1583 then reconstructed in 1960-1 as a hotel. Its 32m-high tower, Bergfried, survives and provides a marvellous view.

Upstream from Bonn the plain of the Köln-Bonn basin shrinks as the slopes of the Rhenish Schist Uplands crowd in on both sides. The skyline south of Bonn is formed by the **Siebengebirge** (Seven Hills) on the far bank. Although only seven or so hills are visible from points between Köln and Bonn, the Siebengebirge range has nearer thirty of these romantic volcanic peaks. A recommended short trip from Bonn or Godesberg is via the Konrad-Adenauer bridge over the Rhine to join road B42 on the east bank and then upstream to **Königswinter**, 10km (6 miles) from Bonn, and the best point of entry to these hills. The most popular one is the **Drachenfels** (Dragon's Rock), 321m (1,053ft) high, which can be reached on foot, by motorcar or by a rack-and-pinion railway from Königswinter. There is a cliff-top restaurant and a ruined castle, Schloss Drachenburg, which give an impressive view over the Rhine landscape.

Public Transport Option: From Bonn, tram line 64 runs to Königswinter. As from Köln, so too from Bonn there are numerous river boat trips available. One of the most important and popular, covering the nearest upstream stretches of the river, is described in the following chapter.

Additional Information

Places of Interest

Aachen

Cathedral & Treasury
Münsterplatz
Open: summer season Monday
10am-2pm, Tuesday, Wednesday,
Friday, Saturday 10am-6pm,
Thursday 10am-8pm, Sunday
10.30am-5pm. Other seasons daily
10am-5pm except Monday 10am-
2pm. If Domschatzkammer
opening times vary enquire
☎ (0241) 4770940

Ludwig Forum for International Art
Open: Tuesday, Wednesday,
Friday-Sunday 11am-7pm,
Thursday 11am-10pm

Rathaus (Town Hall)
Open: Monday to Friday 8am-1pm,
2-5pm, Saturday and Sunday
10am-1pm, 2-5pm.

*Internazionales Zeitungsmuseum
(Press Museum)*
Pontstr 13
For opening times ☎ 0241 432 4410

Köln

Römisch-Germanisches Museum
Roncalliplatz 4
Open: Tuesday-Sunday 10am-5pm,
Wednesday and Thursday 10am-
8pm.
Roman art and glass

*Wallraf-Richartz Museum/Museum
Ludwig*
Bischofsgartenstr 1
Open: Tuesday-Thursday, 10am-
8pm, Friday-Sunday 10am-6pm.

*Schnütgen Museum of Medieval
Church Art*
Caecilien-strasse
Open: Tuesday-Sunday 10am-5pm.

Dom (Gothic Cathedral)
Open: Monday-Friday 10am-5pm,
Saturday 10am-1pm, Sunday from
1pm.

Roman Praetorium
Below New Town Hall
Open: Tuesday-Sunday 10am-5pm.

*Zoo and Aquarium, Botanic Garden,
Rheinpark*
Konrad-Adenauer-Ufer
Open: daylight hours
Gondola aerial railway links zoo
with Rheinpark

Brühl

Augustusburg (Schloss Brühl)
Open: Tuesday-Sunday, 9am-
12noon, 2-4pm. Closed December,
January. Closed Mondays and
when in use for Federal
Government occasions.

Bonn

Museum of Mineralogy
Poppelsdorf Palace
Open: Wednesday 3-5pm, Sunday
10am-12noon.

Beethoven's Birthplace
Bonngasse 20
Open: Monday-Saturday 10am-
5pm, Sunday 10am-1pm.

Museum Alexander Koenig
Adenauerallee 150
Open: Tuesday-Friday 9am-5pm,
Saturday-Sunday 9am-12.30pm.

Rhineland Museum
Colmantstr 14-16
Open: Tuesday, Thursday 9am-
5pm, Wednesday 9am-8pm, Friday
9am-4pm, Saturday-Sunday 11am-
5pm, Monday closed.

River Excursions

Bonn
Day trips on the Rhine, longer cruises to Basel and Rotterdam, and to river Mosel.

Köln
Popular excursions are day trips on the Rhine, longer cruises to Basel and Rotterdam, and to the river Mosel by the 'white ships' of the Köln-Dusseldorfer German Rhine Line, usually known as KD (pronounced Kah Day).
Information from tour offices, travel offices, or
KD-Anlegestelle
Frankenwerft/Rheingarten
Köln
☎ 0221/21 1864
KD operates services to the main resorts on the Rhine and Mosel and timetables can readily be had in all these places.

Hotels

Aachen
Benelux (garni)
Franzstr 21
☎ 0241 22343
Fairly central; parking available.

Bonn
Sternhotel
Markt 8
☎ 0228 654455
Central, quiet

Bergischer Hof
Münsterplatz 23
☎ 0228 633441
Near cathedral and main station.

Köln
Altstadt Hotel (garni)
Salzgasse 7
☎ 0221 234187
Well-placed for riverboat landing stage.

Restaurants

Aachen
Ratskeller
am Markt (in historic Rathaus)
☎ 35001

Elisenbrunnen
Friedrich-Wilhelm-Platz 13a
☎ 0241 21383

Köln
Weinhaus im Walfisch
Salzgasse 13
☎ 0221 219575
(table reservation essential)

Alt-Köln am Dom
Opposite cathedral
☎ 0221 137471
For meal in beer tavern.

Tourist Information Centres

Aachen
Haus Loewenstein
Am Markt 39
D-5100 Aachen
☎ 0241 1 80 29 60

Bonn
Cassius-Bastei
Münsterstrasse 20
D-5300 Bonn
☎ 0228 773466

Köln
Untere Fettenhenen 9
D-5000 Köln 1
☎ 0221 2 21 33 45

2
KÖLN TO KOBLENZ

As an excursion to Königswinter reveals, the Rhine landscape undergoes a fairly dramatic change south of Bonn. The land alongside the river in the Köln area, which the Germans call the Kölner Bucht (Cologne Gulf), gives way to the beginnings of the Rhine Gorge which extends south as far as Bingen. This is where in prehistoric times the river cut its course through a high, bare, undulating plateau of hard slate-like rock, the Rhenish Schist Uplands. And so today the river's precipitate banks separate the Westerwald and Taunus range on the east from the Eifel and Hunsrück plateau on the west. The scenery is spectacular, with castles and keeps on high cliffs and crags looking down on the narrow channel into which the river's waters are constrained to flow forcefully and deep.

Historically the bare, harsh plateau presented a barrier zone between North Germany and South Germany. The narrow and fierce river channel made navigation difficult for the safe passage of goods; cliffs and precipitous slopes made river-side roads equally precarious. Natural obstacles provided an ideal excuse for the exaction of tolls from traders by practices that sometimes had the gloss of legal protection but very often had none. This was the stretch of river around which Rhineland legend, folk-song and literature grew.

It is helpful for visitors to gain a general impression and orientation of the Rhine in this middle section before they start their excursions to individual places of interest. Most people find the best way to do that is to take a river-boat trip from Köln (or Bonn) as far as Koblenz or even Bingen. (These trips are available from the beginning of April to the end of September in most years. Further information is obtainable locally from ☎ (02 21) 20 88-318.)

In descriptions of what is seen from the ship travelling upstream,

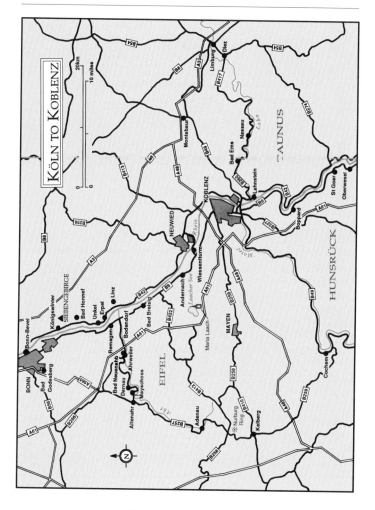

the term 'east bank' will be used for what is seen on the left hand by a person looking forward, and west bank for what is on the right hand; this is to avoid confusion with the geographer's use of 'left bank' or 'right bank' which assumes the convention that the observer is looking downstream.

The ship starts out from the landing stage at the Rheingarten, just upstream of the Hohenzollern bridge in Köln and from midstream there is the classic view of the Dom, Gross St Martin's tower and the

pointed gables of the St Martin Quarter (Altstadt) on the west bank.
Within 2km (1^1/$_4$ miles) the industrial suburb of Porz is passed on
the east bank while the ship navigates a clockwise bend of the river
— offering a fine backward view to Köln as seen beyond the modern
bridge, the Severinsbrücke, suspended by an elegant web from its
single tall, off-centre pillar.

About halfway between Köln and Bonn, on the west bank, is the
industrial town of **Wesseling** with its river-port which handles both
petrochemical products and the brown coal mined west of Köln.

From Köln to Bonn is 33km (20 miles) by river. Facing Bonn (ie on
the east bank) is its industrial suburb of Beuel. Just downstream
before Beuel, the Rhine is joined by its tributary the Sieg, which flows
from the Westerwald hill country east of the Rhine — a favourite
recreational region with many little health resorts. The most important of these is **Siegburg**, lying only 10km (6 miles) from the Rhine.

Six kilometres (4 miles) upstream from Bonn, on the same side, is
the conical hill (122m, 400ft) on which stands the unmistakable tower
of Godesburg Castle, to the south of **Bad Godesberg**, facing across
the river to the Siebengebirge, the Rhine-side outriders of the
Westerwald range. Directly opposite Godesberg is the northern part
of **Königswinter**, Niederdollendorf, from which a popular short
excursion is to the picturesque ruins of the Heisterbacherrott
Cistercian abbey church of which only the handsome chancel still
stands. Königswinter itself is a favourite tourist resort, being the
gateway to the Siebengebirge district, Germany's oldest-established
nature park and perhaps her most popular leisure and recreational
area, with no fewer than 60km (37 miles) of walking paths. Three
million visitors a year use Germany's oldest rack-railway to ascend
the Drachenfels (312m, 1,024ft) to visit the ruins of Burg Drachenfels,
destroyed in the Thirty Years' War; and to enjoy the Rhine panorama, including the mid-stream island of Nonnenwerth, on which
there is a convent of Franciscan nuns. The Drachenfels hill is linked
with the Siegfried legend of the killing of a dragon which lived in a
cave there, while the vines grown on the lower slopes produce a red
wine which bears the name of Dragon's Blood. Königswinter itself
has attractive eighteenth-century burgher houses in its main street,
one of which houses the Siebengebirge local museum.

A short way upstream, also lying at the foot of the Drachenfels, is
the picturesque small town of **Rhöndorf** with its half-timbered
houses. Rhöndorf and the neighbouring spa **Bad Honnef** are now
united as Bad Honnef-Rhöndorf. Rhöndorf was the home town of
the famous Federal Chancellor Konrad Adenauer, and his home is
now a museum, at 8 Konrad Adenauer-strasse. Bad Honnef has

rather a unique feature as a spa: it has spa gardens and an open-air mineral water swimming pool situated on the island of Grafenwerth in the middle of the Rhine and linked to the shore by a bridge. Upstream on the same bank are three picturesque villages: **Rheinbreitbach**, set among vineyards and orchards, was host for some time to the brothers Grimm who wrote the famous fairy-tales; old-world **Unkel** has half-timbered houses and the remains of its medieval walls; as does also its neighbour **Erpel** lying at the foot of its cliff.

On the opposite bank to Honnef is **Rolandseck**, a residential suburb of Remagen (further upstream) with a fine situation, wedged in between river and the crag on which is situated the ruin of Rolandsbogen (Roland's Arch) with its dominant view of Honnef and the Siebengebirge.

Remagen itself lies almost across the river from Erpel, just over 20km (13 miles) upstream from Bonn. Once a Celtic settlement and later a Roman fort, it has a number of attractive pieces of Roman-esque building, including the twelfth-century portal of the parish church presbytery. On the hill above the town is the famous pilgrim-age church of St Apollinaris. Originally it was a Romanesque struc-ture on the site of a sixth-century chapel. It was rebuilt in neo-Gothic style in the nineteenth century and the interior was adorned with magnificent large-scale frescoes by gifted painters of that era who were dedicated to a revitalisation of the religious inspiration in art.

Remagen is best known however to English-speakers for the strategic Remagen Bridge which was built by General Ludendorff in 1918, and was taken intact by US forces in March 1945 after failure of an attempt by the Germans to blow it up. This enabled the first Allied bridgehead to be established across the Rhine under the Erpel cliff-face, preparatory to an advance into northern Germany. Ten days later the bridge collapsed. The two massive masonry towers on either river bank which supported it have been kept; one of the pair on the Remagen side is now a Peace Museum.

Three kilometres further upstream from Remagen Bridge the Rhine is joined from the west by its tributary the river Ahr. On the east bank directly opposite the mouth of the Ahr is the colourful little town of **Linz am Rhein**, a popular calling place for the Rhine excursion ships. The colour and harmony of its half-timbered build-ings in the Markt-platz give it a very attractive atmosphere. Two of its fourteenth/fifteenth-century town gates survive, as does the castle keep which was a summer residence of the Archbishop of Köln of the same period. It now houses a fascinating Musik-Museum specialising in collections of mechanical musical instruments such as

The attractive town of Linz am Rhein

One of the numerous ferries across the river Rhine

clocks and musical boxes, musical automata and the like. The town's late-Romanesque parish church of St Martin has some fine frescoes. From it a path runs up to the Kaiserberg (178m, 584ft) from which there is a splendid view over the Rhein and the Eifel hill country and not least of all into the Ahr valley across the river.

The Ahr Valley & The Vorder-Eifel

At this point of an upstream Rhine river excursion it may be convenient to make an excursion up the Ahr valley, which, of all the Rhine's side valleys, many consider to be the most beautiful, varied and romantic in its appeal. For those using public transport, by leaving the vessel at the Remagen landing stage they can take a train (running about hourly) that plies up the Ahr valley from Remagen, where there is a junction with the main international Rhineside line. Following the valley as they do, all trains make stops at the main places described in the Ahr Valley.

Three kilometres (2 miles) south of Remagen turn right into road B226 for entrance to the Ahr valley. The spa of **Bodendorf** is reached after 2km (1$^1/_4$ miles). The countryside between the mouth of the Ahr and Bodendorf, and stretching to Bad Neuenahr, is known as 'The

Golden Mile' not without good reason. Fields of grain, fruit orchards and rich pastures flourish here on the banks of the river which is joined by trout streams from little side valleys that present an idyllic picture in pastel colours with willows and alders. But as the road climbs the middle section of the Ahr it shows a decided contrast in character: precipitate, rugged and fissured crags and rockfaces obstruct the stream and force it into abrupt twists and bends that make a very dramatic landscape.

From gentle Bodendorf, then, by way of the Apollinaris mineral springs (source of the bottled mineral water, known world-wide, that is shipped from Remagen), the thermal spa resort of Bad Neuenahr-Ahrweiler is reached 12km ($7^1/_2$ miles) further on. The twin resorts both straddle the river Ahr and have merged into one. At the **Bad Neuenahr** end *Kurkliniks* (spa clinics), *Kurhotels*, sanatoria, sports complexes and swimming pools predominate. South of the river is the splendid church of St Willibrord, a tenth-century foundation with a late twelfth-century tower. Beethovenstrasse, flanked by *Kurhotels* and clinics, leads to the baroque residence where the composer spent holidays in the late eighteenth century. Not far away is the *Kurhaus* and Germany's largest casino. (A gaming establishment — sometimes bluntly described as a *Spielbank* but more often associated with a ballroom or similar recreational halls to form a *Kursaal* or *Kurhaus* — is a regular feature of many spa towns.)

Ahrweiler has conserved more of its medieval past than its twin. It has still a good mile ($1^1/_2$ km) of town walls, 7m (23ft) high, from the fourteenth and fifteenth centuries, complete with rampart walks, towers and gates — including two impressive town gates with sixteenth-century sculpted reliefs. The former moat has been transformed into garden parks. All these features give a special attraction to the old town, as do the half-timbered houses. St Laurentius church is of thirteenth-century origin and has interesting frescoes. The Weisser Turm (White Tower) now houses the regional Ahrgau-Museum. The valley is noted for its red wines. And in Ahrweiler the Haus des Ahrweines (Ahr-wine House) enables visitors to taste red wines from the whole valley. There is also a wine museum. The twin town is bounded on the north with south-facing vineyards, through which winds a red wine trail for cyclists or walkers; part of it takes the form of a *Weinlehrpfad*, a trail for instruction in wine.

For most the term 'German wine' is regarded as virtually synonymous with white wine. Admittedly white wines predominate in the German winelands and the most distinguished of them are known throughout the world by their village- and vineyard-name. Yet one or two German areas actually specialise in red wines. One of these is the valley of the Ahr. Indeed it not only specialises in red wines but does so exclusively. So for the motorist the key route to this landscape is the Ahr valley's Rotweinstrasse (Red Wine Road). As the valley runs west to east, not surprisingly the vineyards consistently clothe the south-facing slopes on the river's north bank; the southern slopes are generally wooded. Two varieties of wine-grapes are grown: on the best sites with deep fertile soil and exposure to the sun, the Spätburgunder vine (the *pinoit noir* of Burgundy which has in fact been grown on the Ahr for five centuries) produces deep red wines of high potential; on less propitious sites the Blue Portugesier (which despite its name is credited with having come originally from the Danube region to Germany) produces light, agreeable and mild carafe wines.

The other district in the Rhineland that is noted for its red wines is Assmannshausen, near Rüdesheim-am-Rhein (see Chapter 4).

Leaving Ahrweiler take road B267 for the next stretch which leads into the most impressive part of the rocky valley, as the road — and also the railway — continues 8km (5 miles) to **Walporzheim**, a name familiar to enthusiasts for German red wines. Here there is a wine-pressing house of 1717 date; also the historic wine house 'St Peter' dating from 1246, its name reflecting the connection with the wine estate of Cologne cathedral.

The road's path winds through wine villages such as **Dernau** (where the railway terminates) and **Mayschoss**, where the medieval village's dramatic situation amid craggy rocks seems oddly out of keeping with its winegrowing reputation. After traversing many more vineyards in the course of a further 11km (7 miles) it reaches **Altenahr**, the climax of the journey. Here the stern landscape is shaped by cliff faces and steep crags. The vines grow in stony, slatey vineyard terraces nestling at awkward angles in the rockfaces that dominate the river. A favourite with climbers and hill walkers, this little town also has town gates surviving from its old walls. A bird's-eye view of it nestling between river and crags can be had by taking the chair lift to the Ubigsberg summit.

For those who are travelling by car the Ahr valley excursion can be extended into a round trip that gives a fair sample of the Vorder-Eifel, the nearer part of the plateau lying in the angle between Rhine and Mosel rivers. The excursion could start in Köln or Bonn, if so desired, by motoring south to Remagen on road B9, 39km (18 miles) from Bonn. From Remagen to Altenahr by B226 and B227 is as just described. From Altenahr (which lies at an altitude of 170m, 558ft) at the road fork leave the Ahr valley and take road B257 south to **Adenau**, a picturesque little town in the folds of the Eifel at an altitude of 300m (984ft) not far from the Hohe Acht (747m, 2,450ft) one of the Vorder-Eifel's prominent heights. Adenau has a thirteenth-century basilica for its parish church, and has half-timbered fifteenth- and sixteenth-century houses in its Markt-platz, among them a historic inn Haus-Blaue Ecke (1578) at No 4 Markt. But above all it is probably best known as the nearest township to the Nürburgring race tracks, where more than sixty motor races (both for professional and amateur drivers) take place each year. Grandstands, parking lots and catering facilities are geared to cope with visitors and spectators from far and wide. Nowadays two circuits exist, the original North Loop and the Grand Prix track. Many visiting enthusiasts take advantage of the opportunities which exist to drive their own car or motor cycle over one or other circuit — or to be driven by truck or racing-taxi for a tour of the Ring. There is also the Nürburgring Rennsportmuseum (Museum of Motor-racing).

From Adenau road B257 reaches **Kelberg** in 8km (5 miles), a small climatic and sports resort at an altitude of 490m (1,607ft). From Kelberg roads B410 and B258 lead to the considerable town of **Mayen**. Of Roman origin (when it was known as *Megina*), all that survives of its ancient walls are two gates, at opposite ends, the Brückentor and the Obertor. But the most interesting feature of Mayen is the castle which overhangs the town, the Genoveva Burg with its four mighty towers. Of these, the round tower, Goloturm, 32m (105ft) high, gives a splendid view over Mayen and the volcanic Eifel landscape. The castle also houses the Eifel Museum. Apart from items bearing on Eifel culture in celtic, Roman and medieval times, this museum has geological collections of very special interest. For from time immemorial basaltic lava has been quarried and worked in this neighbourhood, which even met the needs of the Romans for millstones and grindstones. To the north-west of the town a few kilometres away is another old castle, Schloss Bürresheim, situated in its lonely valley like something from a Grimms' fairy-tale. Built as a keep in the twelfth century it was developed and extended as a castle in the fifteenth; it was further developed in the seventeenth century into an aristocratic residence and furnished accordingly; today it reflects the style of life and surroundings of the Rhineland nobility who lived in it until 1938.

Returning to Mayen take road B256 east for 7km, then turning left pick up the sign-post for **Maria Laach** or Laacher See (17km, $10^1/_2$ miles). The Laacher See is the most impressive of the *Maaren*, the ancient volcanic craters of the Eifel that have filled with water to become lakes. Its shore length is 8km (5 miles) and its depth in places is believed to be 52m (170ft). The Benedictine Abbey on the peaceful,

The castle at Mayen makes an imposing backcloth to the town's fair

wooded south-western shore of this austere, indeed almost eerie, waterscape has an abbey-church that is regarded as one of Germany's most important medieval buildings, an exquisitely proportioned six-towered Romanesque church founded in 1093. It is entered through a vestibule known as 'Paradise' distinguished by beautiful sculpted masonry work. The mighty interior's disciplined architecture is all the more impressive for the austere absence of decoration — other than the magnificent high altar with its six-pillared canopy and the carved and painted woodwork that adorns the tomb of the founder, Count Palatine Heinrich II.

From the Laacher See head north-east to the little spa **Bad Tönisstein** in the valley of the river Brohl and thereafter follow road B214 down-stream to the small industrial town of Brohl-Lützing on the Rhine-side road B9, 7km ($4^1/_2$ miles) north of Andernach. To return to Remagen drive north on B9 for 24km, (15 miles).

Remagen to Koblenz

Resuming the river excursion at Remagen, the next calling place is on the opposite bank 5km (3 miles) beyond Linz at **Bad Hönningen**, a small spa on the fringe of the Westerwald Nature Park, having several alkaline thermal springs. On the river front there is, as well as an indoor thermal pool, also an open-air swimming pool fed from the thermal springs.

Two and half kilometres ($1^1/_2$ miles) upstream from Bad Hönningen is the pretty little wine town of **Rheinbrohl** with typical Rhineland half-timbered houses. It once had a very important historical role. Just outside the village was where the Romans made the starting point of an immense system of frontier defences to make the Rhine the eastern frontier of their realm. As the river had tended to become a communication between its two banks rather than a barrier, they had decided to make their frontier zone — in Latin called a *limes* — on the far bank. The system originated by the Emperor Domitian was based on defence in depth. The heavily-armed legionary forces were kept at strong strategic points in the rear, while a 'trip-wire' line was set up well to the east of the river. This consisted originally of a bulky palisade, backed by a deep trench, and with a line of watch towers within sight of one another. This line ran from Rheinbrohl through the verges of the Westerwald, the Taunus and via the upper-waters of the rivers Main and Neckar as far as the Danube near Regensburg. Later emperors replaced the wood-and-earth defences with stone. The *limes* served its purpose for three centuries. Today from Rheinbrohl it is possible to visit remains and even reconstructed parts of the *limes* in this area.

(Consult the information office at the townhall, 9am to 12noon).

Facing Bad Hönningen, on the west bank of the river is another small spa town, **Bad Breisig**, which is very popular with patients suffering from heart or metabolic disorders. It too has many attractive residential buildings of seventeenth- and eighteenth-century date. Two kilometres ($1^1/_4$ miles) south of Breisig is Rheineck Castle on its 182m (600ft) high peak, a nineteenth-century reconstruction on an older site. Here was once a strong-point of the Counts of the Rhine Palatinate which the French destroyed in Louis XIV's 1689 campaign of aggrandisement into the Rhineland.

Eight kilometres (5 miles) upstream from Rheineck lies the substantial old-world town of **Andernach**. Its Rhine-front landmark is its Alter Krahnen — an ancient town crane (with an 8m, 26ft, long derrick) operated by a treadmill in a sixteenth-century round house adorned with Gothic reliefs. For centuries (until 1911) it loaded into river vessels the millstones that were quarried in the Eifel. Andernach is a fascinating place for exploration. As well as some remnants of town ramparts there are two surviving medieval defensive towers. One of these forms the Rhine Gate (dating from around 1200) from the river bank. It is renowned for the Romanesque sculpted figures that adorn it — representing two apprentice bakers who, according to legend, scattered would-be night-time invaders by heaving bee hives upon them from the tower. The other, the Round Tower, a sturdy fortification (yet with surprisingly delicate pinnacle decoration) that withstood French attempts to blow it up, now serves rather romantically as a youth hostel.

Another interesting building is the Altes Rathaus built between 1561 and 1581 with a façade built two centuries later to face onto the Hochstrasse. In the early medieval period it had been the synagogue of the Jewish community; and in its courtyard is preserved the ancient Jewish ceremonial bath, the *Mikwe*. The Mariendom, the Catholic parish church of Our Lady's Ascension, was built around the year 1200, and has many attractive features of architecture. On Koblenzerstrasse that heads south out of town stand the extensive ruins of the Stadtburg, the town castle of the Elector Prince Archbishops of Köln, complete with its Powder Tower. Although blown up by the French in 1689 it still ranks among the best-preserved city fortifications on the middle Rhine. The Haus von der Leyen towards the south end of the Hochstrasse is a good example of a sixteenth-century palatial town residence. It now houses the local museum of antiquities.

But Andernach does not live wholly for its past. Its Mittelrheinhalle, not far from the Alter Krahnen, is a modern civic centre, built in the 1970s, with hotel restaurant, and other facilities. A modern pedestrian shopping precinct fits quite harmoniously into the medieval townscape. A sports complex, with stadium, indoor and outdoor swimming baths, lies on the southern fringe, while to the north is the Stadtwald, ideal for walking and hillwalking. From Andernach a good variety of excursions is available by river boats, train and local bus services. A particularly interesting one that can be carried out by local bus is to the Benedictine Abbey of Maria Laach.

The part of the high, bare Eifel plateau to the west here is known sometimes as the Vulkaneifel, the volcanic Eifel. Its rather desolate rolling landscape is pock-marked with conical basaltic hills that are the cores of one-time active volcanoes. Other prehistoric volcanoes not merely erupted but exploded and in the Eifel are the craters and funnel-shaped depressions that resulted, many of them filled with water to became lakes. One of the most impressive is the Laacher See. It is reached from Andernach by taking the road B9 downstream, past the Alter Krahnen and the slopes of the Stadtwald, then the residential suburb of Namedy (where the former island, Namedyer Werth, lies offshore) to the small industrial town of **Brohl-Lützing**, 7km (4$^1/_2$ miles) from Andernach. Here turn left taking the road B412 up the valley of the Brohl stream and via the little spa of **Bad Tönisstein** to the Laacher See and the Benedictine Abbey on its south-western shores. Its abbey-church, regarded as one of Germany's most important medieval buildings, has already been described in the road excursion in the Eifel.

Public Transport Options. Bus excursions are readily available from Andernach and other Rhine resorts for visits to Maria Laach. The Ahr valley excursions can also be carried out by German Rail services from Remagen to Bad Neuenahr, Ahrweiler, Walporzheim, Mayschoss and Altenahr (DB Timetable No 601). From Andernach the railway runs to Mayen (Timetable No 602).

Four kilometres (2$^1/_2$ miles) upstream from Andernach is a medieval white tower (a one-time toll collecting point) which gives the name of **Weissenthurm** to a small industrial town with several productive breweries. After another 15km (9 miles) the mouth of the river Mosel is reached. The city of Koblenz (French form Coblence) is situated here, very largely in the angle formed by the upstream banks of the two rivers, whose 'confluence' provided the Roman name from which modern Koblenz/Coblence is derived.

A corner of the Weindorf, Koblenz

Koblenz

The tip of the tongue of land in the acute angle between the Mosel and Rhine is known as **Deutsches Eck** — the German Corner. The name derives from the fact that the land here was received in 1216 as an endowment by the Deutschordensritter, the German (or Teutonic) Order of Knights. All that remains of their headquarters and fortress now is a dignified former administrative building and charming formal gardens. Where the point of land juts furthest out a memorial to the Emperor Wilhelm I was erected in 1897. It was badly damaged at the end of World War II, but in 1953 was reconstructed as a memorial to Germany unity. This is the most suitable place to begin a short walk in Koblenz, as it is within a short distance of the Rhine-ships' landing stage. By climbing the pedestal of the memorial a breath-taking view is obtained; and if any one direction of view is more impressive than the others, it must be that across to the east bank of the Rhine where the fortress of Ehrenbreitstein looks down from its dominant site.

Just south of the memorial stands a stately Romanesque church, the St Kastor-kirche founded in the ninth century (the present-day building however being largely twelfth and thirteenth century). The heyday of Koblenz was when the Elector Prince-Archbishops of Trier had residence here. And most of the heritage of these centuries lies close to the Mosel between the Deutsches Eck memorial and the first, many-arched bridge upstream. Walk then along the Peter-Allmeier-Ufer on the river bank to the Deutscher Kaiser, once a sixteenth-century residential tower, now a popular inn for rendez-vous over a glass of wine. From there turn left by Kornfort then right into the Danne past (on the right) the twelfth-century Florins-kirche (St Florian's) and into the pedestrian precinct of Florinsmarkt. There stands one of the old town's most charming groups of build-ings, the Altes Kaufhaus (merchant house) of 1419 and the adjoining Schöffenhaus (aldermen's house) of 1530.

The Altes Kaufhaus now houses the **Mittelrhein-Museum** with its fascinating collections of items illustrating the prehistory and his-tory of the region. A short detour in the opposite direction leads to the Liebfrauenkirche (Church of Our Lady), a colourful and success-ful blend of Romanesque, Gothic and Baroque features. But perhaps even for this historic Altstadt the most evocative items are found on returning from the Liebfrauenkirche and walking along Burgstrasse to the Moselbrücke corner. There stands the **Alte Burg**, a historic castle keep of the thirteenth century. It was originally built by a ruling Trier Elector Prince to suppress Koblenz's ambitions for independence; it was later harmoniously developed into a residential palace with features in Renaissance and Baroque styles. It is notable for its fine, richly decorated spiral staircase. Close by is the oldest of the Mosel bridges, the Balduinbrücke, a masterpiece of medieval building, erected in the mid-fourteenth century by Elector and Prince-Archbishop Balduin. Originally it had thirteen arches, since 1975 only ten. But however old the Balduinbrücke, it was by no means the first at this point; in 1864 the remains of a Roman pile bridge were found only 50m (164ft) further upstream.

On leaving the Mosel bridge the return to the Rhine bank through the Altstadt can be varied by walking south from the Florinsplatz to the neighbouring square, the Münzplatz (Mint Square), where only the Mint Master's House of 1763 survives to remind that once the Prince Elector struck his own coinage here. The square is in any case an inviting place to take a seat under a café parasol for refreshment as well as reflection. Head south again from the square on the Marktstrasse. You shortly reach the crescent-shaped Graben (on the line of a former defensive moat). Turn left and almost immediately is Am Plan square, once a place of execution and a tournament arena, now a favourite meeting place on the edge of the Altstadt. On its north side is the Altes Rathaus. From the Plan continue on the crescent, past the present-day town hall and former Jesuit monastery into Jesuitenplatz from which Firmungstrasse and its continuation Rheinstrasse lead back to the Rhine bank, Adenauer-Ufer, near the *Auskunftsbüro* (information office) open June to end September, the Rhine-ship landing stages and the cross-Rhine passenger ferry station. Just a step upstream is one of the river-front landmarks, the Rheinkran, a former loading crane (built in 1610), now the site of a cafeteria and tourists' rendezvous, which provides a welcome pause before a stroll upstream.

The Rheinkran marks the start of the Augusta-Anlagen, the Rhine-bank gardens. Immediately behind the first section of the gardens stretch the grounds of the neo-classical building of the **Kurfürstliches Schloss**, the Prince-Electors' Palace, the last royal palace built on the Middle Rhine before the French Revolution. After the defeat of Napoleon, when the Rhineland became part of Prussia, it was the Residence of the Prussian Military Governor, Prince Wilhelm who later became Kaiser.

If you continue along the Rhine gardens, passing under the Pfaffendorfer bridge, you see that Koblenz is not given over entirely to historical city sights and memorials. Here is the evidence to support the Rhinelander's reputation for joviality and *Gemütlichkeit* — the famed **Koblenzer Weindorf**, or wine village. At this group of half-timbered houses around a courtyard shaded by chestnut trees,

Rhine and Mosel wines from well known villages are served — and mostly to an accompaniment of food and appropriate music. (Wine tastings for groups can be laid on in advance ☎ 3 16 80 or 3 65 42.)

The part of Koblenz across the river Rhine is not to be missed, especially the fortress of **Ehrenbreitstein**. It can be reached in various ways, by bus, train, or on foot. The simplest way after or before a walk round the old town is to use the passenger ferry from the neighbourhood of the Rheinkran, near Deutsches Eck and the Rhein-ship landing piers. Once across the river and having passed under the railway bridge into the Hofstrasse the ascent to the castle is a little downstream. A chairlift is available and its bottom station is well indicated (bottom station office: ☎ 7 37 66). It can also be reached by car.

The castle of Ehrenbreitstein was in the hands of the Trier Archbishop from the eleventh century, and in the eighteenth century it was held to be one of the strongest on the Rhein. The present-day fortifications were built by the Prussians in 1817-28, after they took over the Rhineland, and their neo-classical architecture had many admirers. In fact, despite its massive size and military purpose it fits well into the Rhine panorama. Today it houses two museums — the

The castle of Ehrenbreitstein at Koblenz

Castles and Keeps

Even those who know the Rhineland well can be surprised to learn how many castles there are. In the Rhineland-Pfalz, the area covered by most of this book, there are 277 listed officially.

In the medieval period castle building became important not just for territorial magnates and nobility but for the whole population. The castles served not only the purposes of the lords who held control over a district — but they also protected its ordinary inhabitants. In the case of a river valley it provided for the safe passage of travellers and goods.

The local magnates who owned lands and castle exacted tolls from traders for their protection. At times this 'protection' acquired the same overtones of abuse as in some places in more modern times. Every district of the Rhineland has its tales of *Raubritter*, or 'robber barons'.

Life in the medieval castle — even for the noblity — was fairly primitive. Comfort was always subordinate to strength and security of the structure. For instance, castle dwellers usually wore furs, not for fashion or display but because castle windows were covered with wooden shutters, not with glass.

The development of gunpowder and cannon brought change. Very few castles were redeveloped to withstand cannon fire. Most of the castles destroyed by Louis XIV's late seventeenth-century invasion remained picturesque ruins. Rulers and local lords erected buildings which were more like palaces than defensive castles. But some surviving castles from the earlier period were transformed as far as was possible into more comfortable residences. With the coming of the Romantic movement in literature and art at the end of the eighteenth century, with its nostalgia for the age of chivalry, many castles were reconstructed to fulfil a romantic fantasy — the style now associated with Disneyland.

All of these are to be found in the Rhineland *Schloss* or *Burg*. Nowadays these words are used without discrimination. But originally a *Burg* was primarily a defensive, fortified structure placed on a cliff or similar site to aid the defenders; it usually started with a straightforward tower-like keep. A *Schloss*, although also defensive, was more elaborate with more emphasis on its residential role. Sometimes it continued to be called a *Schloss* in later centuries when its original defensive structures had been done away with and the buildings, both in purpose and appearance, had become a manor-house or even a palace.

Landesmuseum (provincial museum) and the Rheinmuseum. The former has exhibits illustrating equipment for wine production, stone quarrying, pewter casting, and other old-established Rhineland industries. The Rheinmuseum illustrates the history and practices of river fishing, and the development of shipping on the Rhine from celtic and Roman times to the present-day technical equipment used on the river. The museums are interesting (entry is free), the views from the fortress are magnificent, and the building also houses a youth hostel (*Jugendherberge*).

Koblenz caters for all types of recreation: musical performances of all kinds, theatre, and virtually all branches of sport.

Like most towns on the Rhine and Mosel it has its festive days. Its greatest festival is known as '*Rhein in Flammen*' (Rhine in Flames). On the second Saturday of August a spectacular pyrotechnic display is held which illuminates the Rhine, its banks, castles, villages and towns between Koblenz and Braubach (13km, 8 miles upstream) with fireworks, finishing with a brilliant set-piece in Koblenz.

Visitors with an enthusiasm for camping are likely to be impressed by the main camping site for the city. This is in the suburb called Lützel on the north bank of the Mosel between the Balduin-brücke and the mouth of the Mosel, ie, directly across the Mosel from Deutsches Eck, just where the passenger ferry plies between the two banks.

In the same district of Lützel is the **Wehrtechnische Studiensammlung** (collection of technical military exhibits) maintained by the Federal German Office of Military Technology and Procurement, and fascinating for those interested in military equipment.

Because of its strategic situation on the Middle Rhine with an excellent network of lines of communication in all directions, there is a profuse choice of excursions from Koblenz. Needless to say there is almost an embarassment of river-ship excursions, both on the Rhine and Mosel, and varying from a few hours to several days, when cruise ships travel to Holland or Switzerland.

From Koblenz there is the choice of either continuing the journey (whether by river-boat, road or rail) upstream into the Rhine Gorge or of first travelling upstream on the river Mosel. Many of the vessels that operate Rhine cruises of some days' duration include at this juncture a voyage into the river Mosel as far, at least, as the section generally known as the Lower Mosel, from Koblenz to Cochem. But first there is a worthwhile detour up the Lahn valley.

The Valley of the Lahn to Bad Ems and Limburg

Only 6km (4 miles) upstream from Ehrenbreitstein on the west bank is **Schloss Stolzenfels**, on a bluff facing the mouth of the river Lahn, a tributary of the Rhine. The castle is reached by a 15 minute walk from the town below. Its history goes back to the thirteenth century when it was built to extract tolls from Rhine shipping — and to hold on to the proceeds with the help of a strong keep, drawbridge and fortified gateway, typical of unruly times. Sacked in 1689 by the French, by 1823 it was a ruin. The city of Koblenz made a present of it to their Prussian King Friedrich Wilhelm, and he had it rebuilt with the services of the best architects of the day who made it a principal monument of romantic architecture on the Rhine, with carefully planned visual effects. As such it is well worth a visit.

Opposite is **Lahnstein**, a twin-town situated on both banks of the mouth of the Lahn. Both Niederlahnstein, on the north side of the river mouth and Oberlahnstein, on the south, have river-ship landing stages. By road from Koblenz the simplest route to Lahnstein is to cross the river by the Pfaffendorfer bridge and turn right onto road B42. Enter Niederlahnstein by Kölnerstrasse. (By so doing you will be able to visit both parts of the twin-town, using Bahnhofstrasse and Brückenstrasse for the river crossing.) Niederlahnstein is of importance today as a road and rail route centre, and historical remains suggest this has long been so. At the river mouth the remains of a Roman fort has been found, presumably there to control passage. And there is evidence that the twelfth-century Johanneskirche (the earliest Middle Rhine example of a galleried church) was built on the site of an earlier one. An interesting feature just east of Niederlahnstein is Allerheiligenberg, All Saints' Hill, (157m, 515ft) with its monastery and pilgrimage church at the top. But probably the most interesting sight is on the other, south, side of the Lahn, where Burg Lahneck looks down on the town. This castle (built around the year 1200) was formerly the northern-most guardian fortress of the Prince-Archbishops of Mainz. Today its massive tower gives a marvellous view over the junction of the Lahn with the Rhine and far over the Eifel and Hunsrück hills to the west. The castle chapel is well worth a visit.

The river Lahn is smaller than the Mosel, but just as the latter separates the Hunsrück from the Eifel, so also the river Lahn separates the Westerwald range to the north from the Taunus to the south. Some 11km (7 miles) from Lahnstein, **Bad Ems** lies in the valley between the hill ranges. This is another historic thermal spa, known and used since Roman times. Indeed the Romans' Rhine-frontier defence zone (the *limes* which ran some distance east of the

The fashionable resort of Bad Ems has many elegant buildings

river) passed through what is now Bad Ems. Under the Roman-esque-style St Martin's church were found remains of fort walls with inscriptions of a cohort of the 22nd Roman legion. But perhaps Bad Ems is best known as the fashionable resort and meeting place of nineteenth-century European royalty and aristocracy. Also it was the dispatch of a telegram by Bismarck from the town which played a part in precipitating the Franco-Prussian War of 1870, which in turn led to the unification of Germany under Prussia. Bad Ems has a great range of facilities for all kinds of sports and recreation — from jogging to rifle shooting and from callisthenics to gambling in the *Spielbank* (casino). Among its many regular events are the illumina-tions on Whit Saturday and the Blumenkorso regarded as one of the biggest floral processions in the world — held on the last Sunday of August; on the preceeding Friday and Saturday there are other celebrations of the traditional St Bartholemaeus Market.

Beyond Bad Ems the road follows closely the line of the river as it twists and turns through picturesque countryside sometimes in rocky defiles, sometimes amid vineyards or meadows with delight-ful little towns and villages such as medieval **Dausenau** and the historic **Wirtshaus an der Lahn**, 'Inn on the Lahn'. Nassau is reached 9km ($5^1/_2$ miles) from Bad Ems. Further on is **Oberndorf**, another idyllic village. Right above it rises the one-time Premonstratensian Abbey Arnstein with its abbey-church of St Mary and St Nicholas. The abbey, with its four towers, stands on a crag among woods, peering over the river. The course of the Lahn along its rock-strewn bed is quite tortuous, and the road leaves the riverside for some 15km (9 miles), returning to it at **Diez**. This is another picturesquely sited little climatic resort with half-timbered dwellings, set in the valley basin at the foot of a crag on which stands the castle of the Princes of Nassau, now an attractive youth hostel.

From Diez it is only $4^1/_2$km (3 miles) to the old cathedral city of **Limburg**, set in its fertile valley hollow, 60km (37 miles) from Koblenz. Its strategic situation at the river crossing and on important trade routes led to the settlement here becoming an important trading and communications centre by the end of the first millenium AD. The early thirteenth-century cathedral set high on a crag above the Lahn is a most impressive Romanesque building with its seven towers and its twin-towered façade. Splendid views can be had from the modern *Autobahn* bridge, looking down on the cathedral and castle; another fine viewpoint is the six-centuries old bridge over the Lahn. The Kornmarkt has charming groupings of half-timbered dwellings with gables and oriel windows facing the street.

Those making this excursion by private transport can avoid returning by the same route and gain an impression of the Westerwald by taking road B49 from Limburg via Staffel to **Montabaur**, 20km ($12^1/_2$ miles) to the north-west. The name of the town goes back to 1225, when the then Trier archbishop returned from the crusades, took over the castle and named it 'Mons Tabor' after Mount Tabor in the Holy Land (and in those days accepted as the Mount of Transfiguration). In the course of time the castle was added to and became more of a manorial residence. But even although today it serves as a very imposing regional administrative centre the original castle-keep is still unmistakable. Both the Schloss and, in the Altstadt, the many splendid examples of renaissance and baroque half-timbered buildings in the Gross Markt, will be found to be well worth the detour.

There is an attractive journey south-west back to Koblenz by road B49 via Neuhausel (24km, 15 miles).

Public Transport Option: The excursion to the Lahn valley as far as Limburg can be taken by railway from Koblenz (DB Timetable No 540), the average journey time being an hour; even express trains make stops at Lahnstein, Bad Ems, Nassau and Diez, and the others also at Dausenau and Oberndorf. The railway closely follows the picturesque course of the river. From Limburg, in turn, there is a train service (DB Timetable 423) that reaches Montabaur in about fifty minutes.

Additional Information

Places of Interest

Adenau
Rennsportmuseum
(motor-racing museum)
Nürburgring
Open: March to October daily
10am-6pm, November to February
daily except Monday 10am-5pm.

Andernach
Haus von der Leyen
(Stadtmuseum — museum of antiquities)
Open: Tuesday to Friday 10am-12noon, 2-5pm, Saturday-Sunday 2-4pm.

Bad Ems
Ortsmuseum (local museum)
Rathaus
Open: April to September, Monday and Wednesday 2-5pm, Friday 10am-12noon, 2-5pm; October to March, Friday 2-5pm.

Bad Neuenahr
Ahrgau-Museum
Ahrweiler Weisser Turm (White Tower)
Open: summer Tuesday and Friday 10am-12noon, 2-6pm; Sunday 10am-12noon.

Wine Museum
Himmelsbürgerstr
Open: Sunday 10am-12noon,
Wednesday 2-7.30pm.

Koblenz
Mittelrhein-Museum
Florinsmarkt
Open: Tuesday-Saturday 10am-
1pm, 2.30-5.30pm, Sunday 10am-
1pm.

Landesmuseum
Rhein-Museum
Ehrenbreitstein
Open: 21 March-1 November, daily
9am-5pm.

Wehrtechnische Studiensammlung
(Military Technical Collection)
Mayenerstr 85
Lützel
Open: Wednesday to Sunday
9.30am-4.30pm.

Koblenz-Stolzenfels
Schloss Stolzenfels
Schlossmuseum
Stolzenfels Castle
Open: summer 9am-12noon, 2-
5pm; winter 10am-12noon, 2-4pm.
Closed Mondays and all December.

Königswinter
Siebengebirge Museum
Hauptstrasse

Linz am Rhein
Musik-Museum
(mechanical music-instruments)
Burg
Open: April to October daily 2-
5pm, Sunday and holidays 11am-
5pm.

Mayen
Eifeler Landschaftsmuseum
Burg Genoveva
Open: Tuesday-Saturday 9am-
12noon, 2-5pm, Sunday and
holidays 10am-1pm, but May to
October Sunday 11am-5pm.

Schloss Bürresheim
Open: Tuesday-Sunday April- Sept
9am-1pm, 2-6pm; Oct- March 9am-
1pm, 2-5pm. Closed December

Maria Laach
Naturkundemuseum Winfried
Open: daily 9.30am-6pm.

Remagen
Friedensmuseum (Peace Museum:
'Remagen Bridge')
Bridge-tower on Rhine-bank
☎ 02642 21863
Open: April to November daily
10am-5pm.

Hotels

Bad Neuenahr
Hotel Fürstenberg
Mittelstr 4-6
☎ 02641 2317

Koblenz
Hotel Brenner (Garni)
Rizzastrasse 20-22
☎ 0261 32060
Elegant, peaceful, well-placed,
leading hotel.

Kleiner Riesen (Garni)
Rhein-Anlagen 18
☎ 0261 32077
Quiet, riverside situation. Parking.

Restaurants

Bad Neuenahr
Hotel Fürstenberg
Mittelstr 4-6
☎ 02641 2317

Koblenz
Weindorf
Julius-Wegelerstrasse

Tourist Information Offices

Adenau
Rathaus
Krchplatz
D-5488 Adenau
☎ 029691 20 15

Andernach
Laeufstrasse 11
Postfach 1857
D-5470 Andernach
☎ 02632/298 456

Bad Ems
Pavillon
Lahnstrasse 90
D-5427 Bad Ems
☎ 02603 44 88

Bad Neuenahr
Pavillon am Bahnhof
D-5483 Bad Neuenahr
☎ 02641 22 78

Koblenz
Verkehrspavillon
Am Hauptbahnhof
D-5400 Koblenz
☎ 0261 3 13 04

Königswinter
Drachenfelsstr 7
D-5330 Königswinter
☎ 02223 2 10 48

Linz am Rhein
Burgplatz 13
d-5460 Linz am Rhein
☎ 02644 25 26

Remagen
Drususstrasse 10
D-5480 Remagen
☎ 02642 2 55 72

3
THE RIVER MOSEL

The river which the French call the Moselle rises in the High Vosges of France and its upper waters make a northward journey through the Lorraine industrial region around Metz. But it changes its character as well as the pronunciation of its name when it enters Germany where it is known as the Mosel (with the stress accent on the first syllable). For a short distance it forms the German frontier with the Grand Duchy of Luxembourg where its volume is increased by taking in a tributary from the north, the river Sauer, and another from the south, the river Saar. From then on its course takes a general north-easterly direction to join the Rhine at Koblenz. It is very doubtful whether any other river in Europe can compare with it for the serpentine loops and fantastic horseshoe and hairpin bends as it worms its way through the plateau of the Rhenish Schist Uplands to reach the Rhine. Its serpentine course between Trier and Koblenz covers 189km (117 miles) — which is also the length of the riverside road A53 — but the direct distance from Trier to Koblenz is less than half of that, only 91km (57 miles)!

This meandering course forms one of the most picturesque and unspoiled river valleys in Europe, with more than seventy old-fashioned villages and small towns on its shores devoted to the production of wine. The vines grow largely on sites that seem most improbable; improbable firstly because of the steepness of their slopes, and secondly because of the soil on which the vines grow — harsh, flinty stuff made up of the broken-down fragments of the grey slate which is the substance of these hills. This same grey slate is a major component in the building material of walls and of roofs in the towns and villages. It seems to have the property too of catching and reflecting brilliantly the sun's light so that roofs often look like silver rather than slate.

The Mosel valley between Koblenz and Trier, Germany's oldest city, is commonly regarded as falling into three sections: the Untermosel (Lower Mosel) or Zell district from Koblenz to Zell; the Mittelmosel (Middle Mosel) or Bernkastel district; the Obermosel (Upper Mosel) or Trier district, centred on Trier and including the tributaries Ruwer and Saar. These three sections are also recognised officially by the German wine trade.

The Lower Mosel

The Lower Mosel is the least serpentine part of the river's course and it most resembles the parent Rhine which it joins at Koblenz. Travellers on a cruise ship entering the Mosel from Koblenz will probably pay only passing attention to the large motor-powered barges of 1,000-1,500 tons displacement on the river, but until 1965 the Mosel was only navigable by very small pleasure craft, ferries and local fishing boats. It was one of the first large-scale post-war cooperative undertakings by the governments of the two former enemies, France and Germany, to make the river Mosel navigable to vessels of 1,500 tons all the way from the Rhine to the industrial area of French Lorraine. This was achieved by deepening and widening the main channel and by controlling flow and levels by the construction of massive barrages and locks at key positions. The first of these locks can be seen at Koblenz, just upstream on the Mosel from the Neue Moselbrücke, the new bridge carrying road B9.

Only after this canalisation of the river was it possible to travel on the Mosel on large cruise vessels with modern cabin accommodation. Some ply all the way from Koblenz to Trier. Others which undertake Rhine cruises incorporate a side-trip in the Lower Mosel as far as the popular excursion destination of Cochem, avoiding the charming but extremely serpentine middle and upper sections with their locks. Others, while only operating the cruise ship as far as Cochem, arrange an excursion for their passengers by the fascinating and charming Mittel-Mosel riverside road to Trier.

The first of the better-known Lower Mosel wine villages is 11km (7 miles) from Koblenz. **Winningen** lies on road B416 on the north-west bank of the river where the river's first semi-circular long bend provides on its south-facing slopes a favourable exposure for extensive vineyards. Nearby the Mosel is crossed by the bridge which carries the *Autobahn* from the Eifel across to the Hunsrück. Winningen's Hexenbrunnen, (Witches' Fountain), reminds us that events of three-and-a-half centuries ago are not wholly forgotten here, a reminder reinforced by the local belief that witches were burned on the hilltop on the opposite river bank.

At the other end of the river bend lie the twin villages of **Kobern-Gondorf**, Kobern being some 3km (2 miles) downstream from Gondorf, on the same (west) bank. Several examples exist on the Mosel of such twin villages, but mostly they lie on opposite river banks and are linked by a bridge. The visitor to this region soon becomes familiar with its heritage of half-timbered houses. One which is claimed to be the oldest in all the Rhineland and dated 1325, is part of an elegant group of houses in Kobern's Market Square.

This stretch of the Lower Mosel between Koblenz and Cochem is commonly described as the Burgenland — the 'District of Castles and Keeps'. Not that there is any lack of castles further upstream; but this lower stretch has an impressive concentration. Kobern itself is no exception. An ascent through vineyards leads to the ruins of the Niederburg (Lower Castle), of which only the square Romanesque keep still remains standing. It was once the seat of the Lords of Kobern, the last of whom was beheaded in 1536 as a threat to law and order in the realm. Climbing further above the vineyards by way of the Mühlental (Mill Glen) you reach the Oberburg, or Upper Castle. Close by its sturdy keep stands the thirteenth-century St Matthew's Chapel, considered to be a masterpiece of Rhineland late-Romanesque architecture built originally as a shrine for what were reputed to be the earthly remains of the apostle. Gondorf also has a Niederburg and an Oberburg. The paradoxically named Oberburg on the river bank was at one time this region's only *Wasserburg*, or moated castle. It has belonged to the same family, von der Leyen, since the twelfth century.

On the same west bank of the river as Winningen and Kobern the railway line from Koblenz to Trier runs parallel with the road. Its next station is at the village of **Kattenes**. Kattenes is one of a number of Mosel place-names that have come down from Roman times. Kattenes is believed to derive from the Latin *catenae* meaning 'chains' — referring to the chain-boom across the river for the exaction of tolls from vessels in passage. Opposite Kattenes (and linked with it by a passenger ferry) is the little old-world village of **Alken** where the outlines of its medieval fortifications survive. It too has an old Romanesque church with Gothic wall frescoes; the churchyard has an ossuary or charnel house. The village is dominated by the extensive remains of another thirteenth-century castle, Burg Thurant; of its oldest buildings from 1198 two sturdy round towers remain. Built originally by a Count Palatine it was later captured, extended and maintained jointly by the Archbishops of Köln and Trier. The residential areas of the castle are accordingly divided by a transverse wall separating the Köln and Trier sections, each having its own

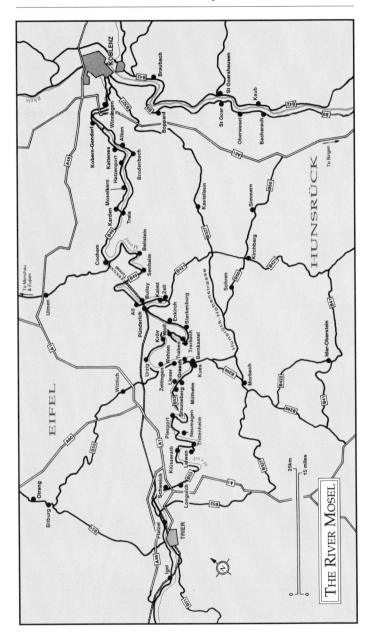

THE RIVER MOSEL

Burg Eltz, hidden in a tributary of the Mosel

gateway — and each also one of the original keeps! Like many other castles and residences in the Rhineland, Thurant was destroyed during the French invasion of 1689 under Louis XIV, but was partially restored in the early twentieth century. Nowadays it houses a collection of arms, paintings and ceramics, and is open all year round.

Further upstream on the same side of the Mosel but confronting the Hunsrück hill country is Ehrenburg, another very notable castle. It stands on a dominating hill-top that can be reached by a side-valley road near **Brodenbach** (about an hour on foot, or 10 minutes by car). It also suffered destruction in 1689 yet is esteemed as one of the most important and impressive ruins in the valley. Built around 1120 and developed from then into the sixteenth century it has many remarkable features including one of the earliest bastion towers in Germany (late fifteenth century) with a spiral ramp for positioning cannon. There is nowadays a hotel at Ehrenburg, open only during the season.

Almost opposite Brodenbach is **Hatzenport** on the north bank. From here is one of the approach roads to a fascinating and unbelievably picturesque castle complex situated north of the Mosel in the valley of its tributary the Eltz in a most dramatic woodland setting. **Burg Eltz** was built in the twelfth to sixteenth centuries, and stands on a steep crag surrounded by beech woods. It is a striking example of a castle shared in common through inheritance by several distinct branches of one family who then developed their four individual residential and defensive buildings around a common inner courtyard. On this restricted site the castle is fortified largely by the precipitous rock faces, the buildings rooted to the very edge of the rock. The buildings rise to eight and ten storeys, their outlines jagged with half-timbered gables and bristling with oriel-turrets at every other corner. Each family-branch has its limits precisely defined, with a few shared facilities, such as chapels and gatetower. The result is a fantastically romantic and picturesque example of a medieval castle.

Burg Eltz was at no time destroyed by hostile action, and so remains probably the finest and best-preserved of the residential castles, having been meticulously restored after a fire in 1920. Still being in the hands of the Count von Eltz's family, its furnishings, paintings, hangings, weapons, gold and silver-work, glass and china are all both authentic and priceless. In the late 1970s a *Schatzkammer*, or treasure chamber, was set up as a museum for the more valuable items of medieval weaponry, sacral vessels in silver and gold of fourteenth- to eighteenth-century craftsmanship and other precious objects of European significance. But apart from the *Schatzkammer* itself, throughout the castle visitors gain a dramatic impression of living circumstances and tastes of the fifteenth- and sixteenth-century Rhineland nobility.

From Hatzenport the route to Burg Eltz takes the form of an interesting detour by way of the little spa town of **Münstermaifeld** (3km, 2 miles) and thence via Wierschem (3km, 2 miles) to the parking place at the Antoniuskapelle (St Anthony Chapel). From here a 15-minute signposted woodland walk leads to the castle, providing en route a dramatically framed view of the castle against a forest background. A glimpse can also be had of Burg Trutzeltz a smaller but menacing counter-fort built by the Trier archbishop overlord as a check on Burg Eltz! From **Müden**, 9km ($5^1/_2$ miles) upstream from Hatzenport, is a much shorter, steeper and tortuous but still charming road leading to an inn from which a 25-minute forest walk takes you to the castle. Finally, hill walkers may wish to tackle the footpath which ascends the valley of the Eltz tributary stream from **Moselkern**, a small village with charming half-timbered houses.

Still on the north bank, 12km ($7^1/_2$ miles) on from Müden, are the 'twin' towns of **Treis-Karden**, Karden lying on the north bank and Treis on the south, linked by a bridge across the Mosel. Upstream from the bridge a good view can be had of one of the Mosel river barrages with its lock. At the bridge the two roads which have served the north and south banks of the river from Koblenz merge. The Mosel Wine Road continues now solely on the north bank for a stretch. Karden is a place of some antiquity, appearing in eighth-century references as *Caradona*, and its architecture has quite a medieval stamp. Its collegiate church of St Castor is a massive twelfth/thirteenth-century building with three mighty towers. To the north is attached a lovely cloister; and the interior of the church has valuable art treasures including a very fine high altar depicting the adoration by the Magi, considered to be one of the best groups of terracotta sculpture of the Middle Rhine region. Among the collegiate buildings is a very fine *Probsteihaus*, or archdeacon's house, and a *Zenth-haus*, or tithe barn, both of early thirteenth-century date. There are fine fifteenth-century wallpaintings in the collegiate school.

From Karden it is but 12km ($7^1/_2$ miles) to **Cochem**, perhaps the best-known of the Untermosel towns, and a regular end-destination of cruise vessels from the Rhine resorts. Cochem marks the end of what has up to now been the fairly straight-line course of the Mosel. Ahead now is the great abrupt loop which is called the Cochemer

A cargo boat heads upstream past the three towers of Karden's church

The Alte Thorschenke built into a medieval gate-tower at Cochem.
The roof is a tribute to the slater's craft

Krampen. It describes a contorted uneven rectangular course such that the upstream headings of the cruise vessel beyond Cochem are, consecutively over a distance of only 28km (17 miles) first south, then east, south-west, south-east, west, north-west, followed by a curve through southwest, south and then south-east to an abrupt turn into a north-west straight for 5km (3 miles), then through a tight loop to the south, again east, and again a straight course for 5km (3 miles) south to the twin towns of Alf-Bullay. Little wonder that the railway line, which accompanies the riverside road from Koblenz as far as Cochem, parts company there and enters the 4km (2¹/₂ mile) Kaiser Wilhelm tunnel to make its own direct way through the slatey rock towards Bullay.

Cochem's emblem, conspicuously high above the town, is the medieval castle, for long a *Reichsburg*, or imperial strong point for the German emperors. In 1294 it came into the possession of the Prince Electors of Trier. It was stormed, despoiled and largely destroyed by the French in 1689, but handsomely restored in romantic neo-Gothic style two centuries later. The ascent from the town takes about 15 minutes, and the interior furnishings and decor well merit a visit — as of course do the magnificent viewpoints over the town, the Mosel and the Hunsrück. Cochem still has three well preserved, fortified

The ferry across the Mosel to Beilstein

town gates one of which is within sight of the ship landing stage on the river front, the Endert-tor, dated 1332; onto it is joined a historic stage-coach inn, the Alte Thorschenke, now a hotel/restaurant of high repute, where, if you wish, your bedroom can be one with a traditional four-poster bed. There is an attractive market place with a fountain, handsome half-timbered houses and a fine baroque town hall of 1739. Cochem has extensive provision for the recreation, entertainment and refreshment of its many visitors. A recreation centre, stadium, open-air and indoor pools and yacht harbour lie across the river bridge in Cond, in the neighbourhood of which is also a nature reserve. From Endertstrasse a chair-lift ascends to the Klottener Höhe — a nature park and viewpoint. Cochem is well placed for excursions into the Eifel using road B249, being for instance, just 30km (19 miles) from Nürburgring, the world-famous motor race track.

The tortuous bends of the river assist the vineyards by reducing the effects of wind in the valley. So the wine villages upstream from Cochem, such as Ernst, Ellenz and Ediger-Eller, profit from the river's erratic meander. Eleven kilometres (7 miles) upstream from Cochem on the B49 Wine Road is the Mosel ferry station that serves **Beilstein** on the opposite shore. This old-world village is compact and incredibly picturesque within the shelter of weathered defensive walls, with colourful alleyways, historic inns and a market place cut into the rock face. It has a baroque parish church of 1738 with a late-Gothic Madonna on a side altar and a *Zenth-Haus* (tithe barn) of 1539 that displays the Metternich coat-of-arms.

On the crag above are the ruins of a former *Reichsburg*, or imperial fortress, but for some time before its destruction by the French in 1689 it was the possession of the Austrian Chancellor Count Metternich. Its thirteenth-century five-sided keep is still standing. The whole village looks as though it has been poured neatly into the narrow ledge between the hillside and the river. As it is the best-conserved group of medieval buildings even in this neighbourhood, it is very properly under a strict State conservation order. It presents an irresistible temptation to leave the B49 road and cross on the ferry, or to walk down the gangway from the river vessel to the landing stage beneath the castle ruin.

At the next hairpin loop after Belstein and before Ediger-Eller there are the twin villages of **Senheim-Senhals**, linked by a bridge. In Senheim, on the south shore, is the Schlagkamp-Desoye wine estate which has a wine museum, with the apparatus used in viticulture and in the cellar-processes of winemaking. The museum has wine tasting and can also lay on a light meal of local specialities.

After yet another hairpin bend the B49 road reaches the important little route centres of Alf and Bullay, 21km (13 miles) beyond Beilstein, linked by a key road bridge over the Mosel. **Alf** lies on the B49; **Bullay**, on the opposite shore, is an important station on the Koblenz-Trier railway line. At one time Bullay was the junction of this line with the now long dismantled Moselbahn, a narrow-gauge railway that corkscrewed along the Middle Mosel loops serving all the wine villages from Bullay to Trier. It was affectionately known as the Säufbähnchen, or 'Little Booze Railway'. The reason for the existence of the Moselbahn was that the main railway line after Bullay cuts away from the loops and twists of the valley to take a direct route to Trier, halving the distance. The Moselbahn has been replaced by the Moselbahn-Bus services.

Alf is a little resort where the Mosel roads meet others from the Eifel, the Hunsrück and the Upper Rhine. So it is well-placed to cater for a wide range of excursions in the region. Nearby on a prominence is Burg Arras, a typical castle keep erected in the tenth century by a minor noble family. Destroyed in 1689 but restored in the early twentieth century, it has a noteworthy interior and a museum as well as splendid viewpoints and catering facilities for visitors.

Alf is also the gateway from the Mosel to a particularly charming valley, which lies between the impressive but somewhat eerie landscape of the Eifel *Maaren* (volcanic lakes) and the vine-clad slopes of the meandering Mosel. It is a side valley formed by a little tributary of the Mosel, the Üssbach, which also has a meandering course but through an attractive forest landscape. In its middle section is the stylish little spa of **Bad Bertrich**, tucked into the valley in the shelter of the Falkenlay hill (418m, 1,371ft). The properties of its thermal springs which contain Glauber's-salts were known in Roman times, while in modern times many swear by its value in the treatment of metabolic disorders. Nowadays its Spa Centre is the bath house and the late-baroque palace, built for the spa in the eighteenth century by the last of the Electoral Princes of Trier. The spa's forest swimming pool in an idyllic setting is a favourite place with visitors. An excursion to the town is appreciated by visitors in high summer for the change of atmosphere and of scene. There is a bus service to Bad Bertrich from Bullay (11km, 7 miles) by German Railway, (DB Timetables 6227, 6242). Also many private operators include it in their excursions from the main Mosel towns.

Motorists who have travelled from Koblenz on road B49 now switch to road B53 if they intend to continue on the river banks through the wine villages of the classic Mittelmosel. But before doing so they should cross the river bridge at Bullay to the east bank in order to visit the prominent wine town of **Zell**, the last one on the Untermosel and well known for its *Grosslage* wine, Schwarze Katz ('Black Cat').

Zell is another fascinating little wine town that retains in its narrow alleys charming houses representative of many periods in its history. It still has remnants of its town fortifications, among them the massive Runder Turm (round tower) that stands by the cemetery above the town amid the vineyards — and which, along with the 'Schwarze Katz', serves as its emblem. Right on the town's main street is the Zeller Schloss, the Trier Electoral Prince's twin-towered residential palace dating from the early sixteenth century. It blends late Gothic, early-renaissance and baroque features and still has a great deal of life about it in its modern function as a hotel.

The wine town of Zell-am-Mosel

The Middle Mosel

The visitor who has enjoyed his trip through the Lower Mosel from the Rhine at Koblenz, whether by ship to Cochem, train to Bullay or by road to either, should not assume it has all been seen. Rather consider the Lower Mosel as a delightful introduction to the unique charms of the Middle Mosel. Perhaps the chief appeal is a result of the serpentine meandering course which it has carved through the slate plateau; thanks to these meanders previous generations found its shores unsuitable for the great international railway lines and arterial modern highways such as were built along the Rhine, and, until three decades ago, even the river itself was unsuitable for through river traffic. So its quaint riverside villages, its immense wine gardens on the slopes and orchards by the riverside have kept unsullied their old-world atmosphere. A frequent reaction of first-time visitors is 'This must have been how the Rhine once was before the industrial age'.

After Pünderich station the Koblenz-Trier-Luxembourg railway line disappears from the immediate river valley. Motorists in a hurry and heavy through-traffic vehicles from Koblenz have a choice of fast roads to Trier over the edge of the Eifel or over the Hunsrück. This leaves the Mosel's riverside roads to local traffic and visitors who wish to savour a journey through an enchanting landscape where the perspectives keep changing with each bend and twist of the river. There are actually several of the river's back-to-back loops where passengers from a vessel can be put ashore, climb over the hills that border the river — and down to reach the riverbank on the other side in ample time to be picked up when their ship finally reaches that point. One of these back-to-back loops is encountered very soon after entering the Middle Mosel. The top of the loop lies at the important wine trade centre of Traben-Trarbach, 22km ($13^1/_2$ miles) upstream from Zell. The hill ridge of the 'isthmus' of land lies opposite the wine village of Enkirch 6km (4 miles) downstream from Trarbach, while on the other side it faces the village of Wolf, 6km (4 miles) upstream. The cruise ship has to travel upstream for 12km ($7^1/_2$ miles) while its passengers can cross the ridge. Nearby the remains of Vauban's great masterpiece Fortress Mont Royal, built during Louis XIV's campaigns of 1688-98, are well worth a visit from the Traben side of the twin town.

Enkirch, a distinguished wine village, is one of a handful of Protestant enclaves in the Mosel valley; the temporal rulers of the region for centuries were the Prince Archbishops of Trier and Köln. Very picturesque with its half-timbered houses set on steeply terraced alleys linked by flights of steps, it has a handsome thirteenth-century Gothic Evangelic church, and also an exceptionally interesting and comprehensive village museum (Heimatstuben-Museum) that illustrates local life-styles from prehistoric times onward.

From Enkirch the riverside road to Traben-Trarbach is squeezed into the narrow shelf between river and the high cliff-like hill on which lie the picturesque ruin of Grevenburg (or Grafenburg) Castle built around 1350, seven times destroyed — finally in 1734 — and the cliff-top village of Starkenburg. Alternatively it is worthwhile taking the minor road that climbs up from Enkirch to Starkenburg village and on to Trarbach following the line of an old Roman road. **Starkenburg** is a fascinating old wine village where friendly local *Winzer* (the regional name for wine growers) are ready to show you their work as well as the end-product. From the top of the Starkenburg cliff there are splendid views over the *Mosel-schleife* at Trarbach. (The commonest regional word for a Mosel river loop is *Schleife* from the German verb to 'grind' or 'cut' in an abrasive fashion — being for instance the word for cutting crystal glass or precious stones.) There is also a bird's eye view of the *Mosel-staustufe* — the control dam and lock — opposite Enkirch.

Traben-Trarbach is another twin town linked by a bridge, Trarbach lying on south and Traben on the north shore. The bridge itself is quite striking because of its comparatively modern bridge gate also housing a *Weinschenke* or wine bar) built in *Jugendstil*, the art nouveau style of which a number of other examples exist in the town. The town suffered much destruction of its medieval heritage in a long series of wars over the centuries as the picturesque ruin of the Grevenburg Castle of 1350 illustrates — and even more so the extensive remnants of the great fortress of Mont Royal built by Vauban, Louis XIV's famous military architect, as the strong point of his flank during his campaign of conquest in the Rhinelands. Mont Royal was built on the peninsula formed by the Trarbacher *Mosel-schleife*. Traben-Trarbach has long been an important centre in the wine trade and many of its warehouses bear widely known names. Handsome merchants' and noblemen's houses in the town include the baroque Haus Böcking (Goethe stayed there in 1792) which now houses the interesting Mittel-Mosel Museum. Less expected perhaps is the Icon Centre in the Kautenbach district. The town is well placed to cater for holiday visitors, offering an extensive range of sports and recreational activities. It even has a satellite thermal spa village in a green wooded glen, **Bad Wildstein**, with all the usual therapeutic and recreational facilities. It hosts a large-scale wine festival during the second weekend of July, with public wine tastings in open-air booths, as well as many other festivals during the season.

Mosel Wine

Of all the major wine growing countries, Germany is the most northerly, so minor differences in the micro-climate of its vineyards can influence quite critically the taste of the wine. Such factors as whether they face south, the angle of slope to the sun, what shelter exists from winds, reflection of sunlight from water, are all important. Equally critical is the nature of the soil, which in even the best Mosel vineyards resembles the fragmented debris of a slater's yard! Fortunately, for centuries German winegrowers have fostered the Riesling grape which not only survives but positively thrives in that soil and on its steep slopes, sending its roots in a deep search for humidity and responding to the slatey surface's capacity to store and reflect the sun's warmth. Given the right environment, this grape produces fine wines of subtly fragrant flavour (often, when young, having a *spritzig* or 'tingling' quality). The Riesling grapes are small, and the crop is less prolific than other, blander varieties, so for more than a century German wine-research institutes have sought to breed a variety that has a bigger yield than the Riesling, yet keep its noble qualities. Many new varieties have been tried — some are favoured in other German regions, and some produce table wines on sites with richer 'loamy' soils, but none have yet displaced the Riesling grape.

Quality Clasification of German Wines

With such differences in quality and flavour, how should the visitor choose which wine to buy? Both EEC regulations and German Wine Law insist on a great deal of information being given on wine-labels — too much for some people.

• *Qualitätswein mit Prädikat* 'Wine of Quality with Distinction' which will also bear its individual official test-batch number (*Prüfungs-Nr*). This number indicates checking and tasting at time of bottling by an independent official commission.

• *Qualitätswein bestimmter Anbaugebiete* sometimes abbreviated as *QbA* or 'Wine of Quality from specified districts of production' is the next slightly lower category of fine quality wine., and also has a test-batch number. Germany is unique among wine-producing countries in this rigour of quality control by independently conducted official tests with identifiable index-numbers. *Riesling Hochgewächs* is an additional sub-category introduced to the German Wine Law in 1986 to recognise a superior level of Quality Wines — not *Prädikat* wines. This wine must be made 100 per cent from Riesling grapes; contain a much higher concentration of pressed grape juice than normal Quality Wine and must have a higher rating in the sensory tests at time of bottling (it must score double that of normal Quality Wine.) This category is mostly used in the region Mosel-Saar-Ruwer, where it finds favour for drinking with meals because of its more intense character — until recently the Germans drank the best quality Rhine and Mosel wines socially rather than at meal times.

• *Tafelwein* The next main category — which can be translated as 'quaffing wine' — has no official checking number to indicate quality-testing and merely bears the name of its place of origin or district, eg 'Bernkasteler' or 'Bereich Bernkastel' (district of Bernkastel) and may be a blend from several vineyards in that district and from a mixture of grapes (unless the grape variety is positively stated).

The next thing to look for on the label of a 'Quality' wine is the name of the grape, and if the word 'Riesling' does not appear then the wine is made from some other grape (stated or unstated) or a mixture of varieties. Along-side the grape name, eg Ries-ling (or one of the newer grapes such as Optima, Kerner, or Bacchus) a top

The Riesling grape produces the fine

quality wine will normally also indicate the level of ripeness (as measured by the grape-sugar content in the grape-juice). In ascending order these are: *Kabinett*, *Spätlese* (later harvested and so having a higher level of grape sugar for fermentation), *Auslese* (selectively picked for even greater ripeness). The last mentioned is usually sweet — but it must also have a fruitiness and sharpness to balance such sweetness.

Vineyards and Sites

High up on the label is usually the name of the village, town or parish, in its adjectival form (ie ending in '-er', eg Bernkastel*er*), followed by the name of the site where the grapes were grown.

Each of the 2,600 individual vineyard sites (*Einzel-lage*) in Germany is officially registered by name. What often cause some confusion are the 130 site names that are not of *Einzellagen*, indi-

white wines of the Rhine and Mosel

vidual vineyards, but of what are called *Gross-lagen*, translated as 'Comprehensive sites'. These enable the grower of wine from, say, a well-favoured but lesser-known small vineyard to market his wine (if he wishes) under the name of a larger and more widely-recognised site. In theory wines from the whole of any *Grosslage* are supposed to possess similar characteristics. But not all consumers find this convincing. The area of vineyards that can adopt the *Grosslage* name of 'Piesporter Michelsberg', 'Bernkasteler Kurfürstlay' and 'Zeller Schwarze Katz' extends over many square miles and not all of it on the steep sunny slopes. So it is useful to be able to identify which names are of *Grosslagen* and which of *Einzellagen*. Some examples of *Einzellagen* and *Grosslagen* in the Mosel, Rheingau and Rheinhessen regions are given overleaf.

To buy wine direct from the *Winzer* or wine-grower — and 25 per cent is sold directly to the consumer — look out for *Flaschenweinverkauf*, meaning 'bottled wine sold here'. More obscure is the sign *Strausswirtschaft*, literally 'Garland business' — a reference to the historic practice of indicating wine for sale by hanging out a grapevine garland.

Some Typical Mosel, Rheingau & Rheinhessen Wines

Mosel

Locality	Vineyard (Einzellage)	Grosslage
Bernkastel	Schlossberg	Kurfürstlay
Cochem	Herrenberg	Goldbäumchen
Enkirch	Edelberg	Schwarzlay
Erden	Treppchen	Schwarzlay
Kröv	Herrenberg	Nacktarsch
Piesport	Goldtröpfchen	Michelsberg
Traben-Trarbach	Schlossberg	Schwarzlay
Trier	Domherrenberg	Römerlay
Trittenheim	Altärchen, Apotheke	Michelsberg
Ürzig	Würzgarten	Schwarzlay
Wehlen	Sonnenuhr	Münzlay
Zell	Nussberg	Schwarze Katz
Zeltingen	Himmelreich	Münzlay

Rheingau

Eltville	Taubenberg	Steinmächer
Johannisberg	Vogelsang	Erntebringer

Rheinhessen

Nierstein	Pfaffenkappe	Gutes Domtal
Oppenheim	Schloss, Schlossberg	Krötenbrunnen
Worms	Liebfrauenstift-Kirchenstück	Liebfrauen-Morgen

Wolf, another of Trarbach's satellite villages, is 6km (4 miles) upstream. Its many fine half-timbered buildings look out on a quiet, beautiful river bend just beyond where the riverside through road, B53, turns to cross the river bridge to the north shore. Here the Mosel describes a second tight bend to complete the S-shaped back-to-back loop that started at Enkirch. Almost opposite Wolf are the first of the vineyards belonging to Kröv, one of a trio of famed wine villages where there is a very gentle south-facing curve of the stream, behind which the vine-bearing slopes have a very favourable angle to the sun at all seasons. The villages of **Kröv** and **Ürzig**, with their many medieval half-timbered buildings, lie on the north bank, while **Erden** is on the south, but the noble vineyards of all three are terraced on the northern slopes. The *Winzer* of Erden have to cross the river to attend to their choicest vineyards — such as the 'Erdener Treppchen' whose name *Treppchen* or 'flight of stairs' is a reminder of the steep slopes that have to be climbed after the river is crossed! Such river crossings are quite a commonplace chore on the Mosel; for any patch of the right kind of soil having the right angle of sun exposure is reserved for vines. So if need be, the houses, the church and the churchyard are sited on the less favoured river bank even though bridges or ferries have to be used to get labour and gear to the cultivated slopes facing south.

On a rock face protruding from the Ürzig vineyard slopes are the first of several giant hillside sundials that are emblematic of the *Winzer*'s obsession with sunlight. That motif is repeated when the river's next great sweeping *Schleife* is entered at **Zeltingen**, home of Zeltinger Sonnenuhr ('Sundial') wine as well as of Zeltinger Himmelreich ('Realm of Heaven'). Incidentally, the vines further up the slopes from the Sonnenuhr produce the equally regarded Schlossberg (Castle-hill) wines. They grow on terraces formed from the ruins of a former castle.

Neighbouring **Wehlen** also exports its famed 'Sonnenuhr' wine world wide. And again a great white sundial showing the hours in Roman numbers contrasts with the grey slate rock and the greenery of the vines that grow on the steep slopes across the river from the village — cheering the villagers in autumn with the assurance that the sun is still favouring their crop. The Mosel valley's sole suspension bridge connects these vineyards with their owners in the village across the river. Wehlen has many attractive half-timbered buildings, including a very charming tithe-barn, at a bend on the road down to the suspension bridge. On the same side of the river as the Wehlener sundial is the smaller village of **Graach**, a name perhaps not so widely known as the two just mentioned; yet the wines of Graach, from vineyards lying between Wehlener Sonnenuhr and Bernkastler Badstube can well compete with those of their bigger neighbours.

Bernkastel-Kues, the very heart of the Mittelmosel region, is another of the twin towns linked by a Mosel bridge. The motorist travelling by road B53 from Wehlen (on the west bank) enters first Kues, and as the bridge to Bernkastel is crossed there are three notable landmarks ahead. On the river quay slightly to the left is the impressive fourteenth-century square tower of the Gothic parish church of St Michael with its slated spire flashing in sunlight. Away to the right are the still shapely ruins of the thirteenth-century Landshut Castle that, until the seige of 1692, was one of the realm's great strongholds. Ahead, above the town, are the curves of one of the world's most famed vineyards, the Bernkastler Doctor.

If you come upstream from Zeltingen on the east bank, take the

The vineyard sundial at Zeltingen, home of the Zeltinger Sonnenuhr (sundial) wine

Traben seen from its twin town of Trarbach across the river Mosel

The market place at Bernkastel with its attractive half-timbered buildings

first entrance to the river bank parking place and then walk up the first side street, the Graben, to enter the town through the Graacher-tor, the old-world town gate. In either case the ultimate destination is the most picturesque of all German market places, surrounded by half-timbered houses, a noble late Renaissance 1608 town hall and, nearby, the quaint *Spitzhäuschen* of 1583, a tiny two-storey house with pencil-pointed gable end facing the square. Slightly off-centre but dominating the scene, is the beautiful fountain of 1606 that bears the name of the town's patron saint, St Michael. On the first weekend of September this marketplace is the scene of the greatest Mittel-mosel Wine Festival, where the great 'growths' are sampled at the booths.

Kues, on the other side of the river, is of even greater antiquity than its partner, as an early Stone Age village was excavated there comparatively recently. It gave its name to its greatest son, Cardinal Nikolaus Cusanus, the great medieval polymath and theologian, born here 1401. He founded the St Nikolaus Hospital that still exists today, and was endowed with choice vineyards. It was founded as a home for thirty-three aged paupers; the impressive complex of buildings (standing next to the Mosel bridge on the Kues side) is a fascinating place to visit today with its many treasures, its library and its historic Wine Museum.

On the Kues side of the river, downstream but rather uphill, is an educational and recreational precinct that includes games fields, as well as open-air and indoor swimming pools. In the same vicinity and worth a visit are the huge central wine cellars of the very successful Co-operative of Middle-Mosel Winegrowers. The most up-to-date technology is used and its 'Mosel-land' wines are ex-ported and respected worldwide. Also on the Kues side but up-stream from the Mosel bridge is a camping site and large boat marina.

Excursions from Bernkastel include river vessel trips upstream to Trier and downstream to Traben-Trarbach, Cochem and Koblenz; the Moselbahn-Bus services along the riverside between Trier and Bullay enable trips in both directions to be made from Bernkastel. A linking service by Bahn Bus also runs from Bernkastel to Wittlich-Wengerohr, a station on the Koblenz-Trier main-line railway. Spe-cial excursions during the season are also run to the Eifel lakes, to Luxembourg and to the Hunsrück (a favourite destination being the gem-cutting town of Idar-Oberstein). During high summer, when daytime temperatures are high in the Mittelmosel valley, the Hunsrück offers picnic excursions that tempt motorists to head for its cooler climate.

BERNKASTEL INTO THE HUNSRÜCK

A principal approach to the Hunsrück from many Mittelmosel resorts is the B50 road which climbs up from Bernkastel with many a twist and turn (passing close to Burg Landshut on its way) to reach the village of **Longkamp** after 4km ($2^1/_2$ miles). Shortly after Longkamp, take the B269 road which branches off right to reach the little climatic resort-town of **Morbach**, 17km ($10^1/_2$ miles) from Bernkastel. Here on the plateau it is 335m (1,100ft) above the river. Morbach lies on the important scenic tourist road B237 (European road number E42) known as the *Hunsrückhöhenstrasse* which crosses the Hunsrück plateau in a fairly straight line towards the Rhine and so is a fast road to places such as Boppard, St Goar, Bingen or even Koblenz. It passes through magnificent high forest and farming country, dissected by glens. In the region there is picnicking on the forest fringes and visits to charming country market towns.

Morbach is suggested as a first destination for two reasons. Immediately to the south of it stretches the Hunsrück Nature Park, a fascinating area to visit. Also from Morbach is a most interesting circular excursion to **Idar-Oberstein**. From Morbach take the southward continuation of B289 for 8km (5 miles) as far as the crossroads with the B422 (where on the right the Erbeskopf (818m, 2,684ft) will be seen). Turn left on to the B422 which curves round to reach Idar after 21km (13 miles) by way of the conservation park area and the 'German Gem-stone Road'. This area's economy has long rested on the cutting and polishing of precious stones. When, in the last century, local supplies became practically exhausted, imported raw materials (largely from South America) were used, and the local skills are still much in demand in scores of gem-cutting workshops. However some of the former mines and one of the traditional water-driven mills for grinding and polishing may be seen by visitors. Idar-Oberstein is recognised as Europe's gem-cutting centre, and has many specialised workshops (visits being arranged through the tourist information office) and the unique Deutsches Edelstein-museum (Precious Stone Museum) with exhibits of the world's gem stones, cut and uncut.

The town is also noted for its architectural curiosity, the Felsenkirche, the Church in the Rock, built into a niche in a cliff face, 50m (164ft) above the valley floor and overhung by a vertical rock face. The church, of late fifteenth-century date, has suffered over the years from rock falls. From Idar-Oberstein the return journey continues by road B41 to Birkenfeld (18km, 11 miles) to rejoin the B289 for the northward leg of the route to Morbach, a further 27km (17 miles). The final stage of the return to the Mosel can be varied by leaving the B50,

Tying up the vines to their stakes, on the steep slopes above the Mosel

Burg Landshut stands among the Schlossberg vineyards above Bernkastel

turning left after Longkamp village, and taking the scenic modern road via Monzelfeld that gives high views over the Mosel valley as it sweeps down to regain the riverside at Mülheim, 6km (4 miles) upstream from Bernkastel.

Public Transport Option: During the summer season (June to October) the Moselbahn-Bus company runs a weekly half-day excursion from Bernkastel (and other Mittelmosel resorts) to Idar-Oberstein more or less by the circuit described above, with visits to the Gem Museum and the Felsenkirche. (Details from local tourist offices.)

A modern bridge replaces the ferry that formerly linked **Mülheim** with Lieser on the other shore of the river Mosel. The little wine village of **Lieser** shares the name of a tributary of the Mosel which flows from the Eifel. A few kilometres upstream on the banks of the

The famous Church in the Rock at Idar-Oberstein in the Hunsrück

Lieser stream is a fairly large wine estate with a very interesting history. As the first part of its name reveals Klosterhof Siebenborn was once the wine-producing grange of a monastery — the ancient Cistercian monastery of Himmerod in the Eifel 20km (12 miles) away, founded on the initiative of St Bernhard of Clairvaux in 1178 (and one of two still surviving monasteries of that order in modern Germany). The order's rules allowed a monastery to have satellite farms (or wine estates) so long as these were within a day's journey of the mother church. The Cistercians are credited with making great contributions to development in vine growing and as early as the twelfth century Himmerod monastery had three vessels on the Mosel for the transport of wine downstream as far as the lower Rhine. Along with other religious houses Himmerod was secularized by Napoleon in 1802, and the monastery's Siebenborn estate was acquired in 1844 by the Melsheimer family which still runs it today. Today's wines continue to be laid down in the impressive Romanesque-vaulted cellars which date back to the twelfth century. But the wine-growing traditions here pre-date even the Cistercians. In 1977 improvements to a vineyard access road laid bare an intact, but buried, Roman wine-pressing plant which the archaeologists date to the second century AD. The basin into which the juice drained from the trodden grapes has a capacity of precisely 960 litres (211 gallons). It seems more than a coincidence that this is the capacity of today's traditional Mosel *fuder* cask!

Shortly beyond Mülheim lies the village of **Brauneberg**. Its famous Brauneberg Juffer vineyard lies across the river from the village and the main road; its slopes are probably the steepest of all in the Mittelmosel and have an enviably clear southern exposure. Not surprisingly the Brauneberger Juffer is another of the most distinguished Mosel wines. Twelve kilometres ($7^1/_2$ miles), further on lies the village of **Piesport** backed by its remarkable steep-sided amphitheatre of vineyards facing south on the outer side of another great Mosel loop. Here the cyclist has a great advantage over the motorist. Road B53 surmounts the crest of the slope on which the main village lies, but the well-metalled cycle path hugs the river bank facing the long spectacular amphitheatre of vines that downstream ends in the rock massif that is known as the Mosel-Loreley. The antiquity of this wine village is witnessed by the Roman origin of its name *Pisonis portus*.

You come out of the Piesport river loop to enter the parish of **Neumagen-Dhron** where the most famous of all Roman finds was uncovered. Among a great number of other informative Roman artistic objects found was the *Neumagener Weinschift*, a Roman sculp-

ture representing a Mosel ship carrying a deck cargo of wine casks of
the same shape and the dimensions of the *fuder* cask still used on the
Mosel today. The original sculpture is now in the great State Mu-
seum at Trier; but a fine replica stands in the tiny park garden of the
St Peter's churchyard in Neumagen. Less than a block away stands
another famous Roman sculpture relief of that same era: the
Pachtzinszahlung, a graphic representation of 'The Payment of the
Rents' by tenant farmers.

No less a Roman than the one who later became the Emperor
Constantine the Great is credited with establishing a fort here at
Noviomagus to protect the road from Trier to Mainz, while the
imperial household had a summer villa here. At Neumagen the
Mosel Wine Road B53 crosses the river to run upstream on the west
side of another Mosel loop, passing through the wine villages of
Trittenheim and then — on the reverse of the loop — **Leiwen**, with
finally **Klüsserath** where the river's course is straight again. The
Leiwen-Trittenheim *Schleife* is the tightest long 'hairpin' of all. A fine
view of it can be had from the terrace of the small hotel restaurant
Zummethof on the hillside, above the vineyards, right above the
bend of the loop. From Trittenheim it can be reached by crossing the
river bridge to the east bank — on which lie both Neumagen and
Leiwen — and taking the zigzag hill road heading to Büdlich.

After Klüsserath the section of the river described as the Mittelmosel is considered to end — that is at least the view of most German
wine experts. For they attribute the noble and delicate qualities of the
great Mittelmosel wines, made from Riesling grapes, to the soil from
the slatey rock of the Rhenish Schist Uplands through which which
the river has cut. Upstream from the loop which ends at Klüsserath
the slatey slopes begin to taper down into the great saucer within
which lies the great and ancient city of Trier. However, there are one
or two interesting places before Trier is reached. **Detzem**, for instance, has a name derived from the fact that it stood at the tenth (*ad
decimum*) Roman milestone from Trier. And, some 15km (9 miles)
upstream from Klüsserath, but on the opposite bank, is **Longuich** —
again of Roman derivation (*longus vicus* or long village) — which is
one of the places in this area where the orchards produce *viez*, the
local name for an apple wine. **Pfalzel**, now a suburb of Trier, is 7km
(4 miles) further, the name revealing that it was once the site of a
Roman *palatiolum* or little palace. Before World War II excavations
there revealed one of the several Roman mosaic floors that have been
uncovered in the region around Trier.

On the opposite side of the river to Pfalzel is the mouth of a small
tributary of the Mosel, the Ruwer, a name familiar to many people

because printed on all Mosel wine bottles is the full legal name of the *Anbaugebiet*, or region of production, which is officially 'Mosel-Saar-Ruwer'. The Ruwer valley produces some fine, delicate light wines of which those bearing the village names Kasel and Waldrach may be best known, such as Kaseler Nies'chen or Waldracher Krone.

Trier and Environs

Comparatively few English-speaking travellers visit Trier, one of Europe's most historic, most civilized and most charming smaller cities. Paradoxically Trier was founded and developed great importance because of its key situation as a routes' centre, but when the railways came the great international routes seized on the Rhine valley for penetrating Germany and Trier was rather by-passed. It is ironic that the absence of international railways and fast roads has done much to preserve the old-world charm of the Mosel valley — but has left Trier more ignored by visitors than the city merits.

Trier is Germany's oldest city, having been founded in 16BC by the Romans as *Augusta Treverorum* — 'city of Augustus in the territory of the Treveri tribe'. Its site was of strategic importance where Roman roads from Rheims, Mainz, Lyon and Köln met. When the Roman Empire's frontier was stabilized on the east side of the Rhine, then the Rhine-Mosel region in the secure hinterland west of the Rhine developed as a realm of prosperous Roman urban civilisation and economy, with Trier as its centre. Trier actually became capital of the western part of the Roman empire after the Emperor Diocletian's reorganisations at the end of the third century AD; it also became an imperial residence and six emperors held court here. Its surviving heritage from that era is without parallel anywhere north of the Alps, as even a brief city walk reveals.

The old city centre is largely a pedestrian precinct and a tour on foot is most conveniently started at the massive Roman city gate of the second century, the **Porta Nigra**, the largest and best preserved Roman city gate in the world. It was built of mighty sandstone blocks held together without mortar but with iron clamps. Its name (' The Black Gate') is ascribable to the blackening of the sandstone by age. During the medieval era it was converted for use as the base of a two-storied church of which the Romanesque apse still survives, although the rest of the medieval structural additions have been long demolished. Adjoining the Porta Nigra is an eleventh-century collegiate building, the **Simeonstift**, with two-storied cloisters around a courtyard, the Brunnenhof (Fountain Court), where in summer visitors can sit at café-style tables for refreshment while watching the world go by. The Simeonstift building complex is now the home of

Porta Nigra, the Roman city gate at Trier

The market place in Trier is a pleasant place to relax

the Municipal Museum; it also houses the city's tourist information office. At no great distance in the Simeonstrasse is No 19, a good example of a thirteenth-century residential tower whose entrance was originally one storey up, for security in unruly times.

Simeonstrasse leads into the **Hauptmarkt**, where the sturdy market cross was erected in 958AD as a sign of the city's entitlement to hold markets. Close by is the ornate renaissance St Peter's Fountain. Facing into the marketplace are two unusual buildings: one known as the Steipe (an archaic word meaning a pillar) was a fifteenth-century councillors' banqueting hall. The adjacent Rotes Haus, or Red House, goes back to 1684. The south side of the market is dominated by the steeple tower of the Gothic St Gangolph church.

Half way along the Hauptmarkt the short Sternstrasse goes off at right angles into the Domfreihof, with the **cathedral's** romanesque west façade of eleventh-century date straight ahead. This is a remarkable building, illustrating the unbroken harmonious continuity of ecclesiastic architecture from the Roman era to our own age. The inner kernel is a large and well-preserved part of a Roman building of the late fourth century. Even at that early date (and it was begun in the year 330AD) the impressive structure was designed as a full-scale cathedral. Its foundations rested on the site of the residential palace of the Constantine era. The tradition is that the palace was that of the Empress Helena (mother of Constantine the Great). Indeed, in the course of excavations that were carried out in 1945-6 because of war damage, a number of very beautiful paintings were found and recovered from the ceiling of the Roman palace hall. These included portraits, now in the Episcopal Museum, one of which may depict a member of the Imperial family.

The cathedral's west choir is of eleventh-century construction, while the polygonal east choir and towers are of twelfth-century date. The lovely cloisters however are from the thirteenth century. The centrally planned Holy Robe Chapel was added in 1716 in the Baroque period. Outstanding among the cathedral's possessions are the portable St Andrew's Altar, a specially fine example of the medieval goldsmiths' art, held in the cathedral treasury; and *Der Heilige Rock* or Holy Robe, which tradition relates was the seamless garment of Christ, brought from Rome by the Empress Helena. Finally, in the early eighteenth century the transept was built and large windows brought in the light so characteristic of that period.

Next to the cathedral is the **Liebfrauenkirche** (Church of Our Lady), one of Germany's earliest Gothic churches, which was erected in the mid-thirteenth century to replace a former Roman basilica which had become unsafe. The blending of architectural influences from Germany and France (Soissons and Rheims in Lorraine) contributes a great impression of harmony in the central structure.

Almost opposite at Liebfrauenstrasse 9 is the eighteenth-century residence of the von Kesselstatt family, now as then famed for their wine estates with plots on many distinguished Mosel wine hills. A break for a serious wine tasting can be arranged here.

Continue south along Liebfrauenstrasse to its end. Cross the irregularly-shaped 'square' of Konstantinplatz, passing on the left the Red Tower, to reach the massive tile-built former **Roman Basilica** (often in German called the *Palastaula* or in Latin the *Aula Palatina*), the imperial audience hall of the palace of Constantine's day. This building is a unique survival of its kind and size from the Roman Empire. It is unique also in its history, for in the seventeenth century it was incorporated into the palace of the Electoral Prince Archbishops of Trier, and after having been extended last century to serve as a Protestant church, it has received loving restoration after World War II as the Church of our Redeemer.

This is why the site is shared by a building complex of different styles — the Prince-Elector's Palace in its final seventeenth- and eighteenth-century form, east and north wing in Renaissance style, and the south wing baroque with a striking rococo interior staircase. It is nowadays the seat of the district government. In front of the south wing are the attractive formal palace gardens. On their east side are surviving sections of the medieval city wall which include a former minor city gate, the Kastilport. Beyond the city wall stands the Landesmuseum, or Provincial Museum, with its entrance from the palace gardens. Beyond the gardens, to the south, are the massive and still shapely ruins of the **Kaiserthermen**, the fourth-century Roman bathing establishment which still preserves in stonework the main outline of the hypocaust heating structure.

All this is within walking distance. If you feel energetic continue further east in the direction of the Olewig suburb to the **Amphitheatre** — the ruins of a Roman gladiatorial arena of around 100AD, which is estimated to have catered for 25,000 spectators.

The amphitheatre can be reached by bus, using routes 6, 16 or 26. A useful public transport folder can be had from the tourist information office (along with others in English). They also have information on a guided tour in English at 2pm daily in season, or by private appointment at any time. One of the city bus tours of the sights (information from the tourist office) is a useful preliminary to a leisurely circuit on foot to the places that particularly appeal to you.

At the southern end of the city the **St Matthias** Romanesque abbey-church, dates from the tenth and twelfth centuries, and has the tomb of the apostle. There are also Roman tombs there.

Near the river bank are a number of things worth seeing, including ∏ **Barbara Thermen**, the remains of another Roman bath establishment. A little downstream, ie north, is the Römerbrücke's continuation into the city, Karl-Marx-Strasse which in turn becomes Brückenstrasse. Towards the end, on the left-hand side at No 10, is the **Karl Marx Haus**, now a museum of nine rooms, documenting the life of Marx (who was born here) and the development of socialist thought in the nineteenth century. Nearby too, around the corner, are the ∏ recently excavated **Forum Baths**.

Returning to the Römerbrücke, and continuing downstream, you will see two old-style loading cranes on the quayside. The first, the ✳ Zollkran of 1774, is a replica of the other, der Alte Kran (Old Crane) of 1413. The next bridge downstream is the Kaiser-Wilhelm-Brücke, below which lies a picturesque row of late eighteenth-century fishermen's and boatmen's houses, collectively named Zurlauben. Here is the city's river boat landing stage and harbour, from which in summer local trips are made downstream to Pfalzel. Here too is the ground station of an aerial cable car to the Weisshausterrasse viewpoint on the hill across the river.

Understandably, Trier's historic buildings are complimented by museums of outstanding interest. Passing mention has been made of the **Landesmuseum** at Weimarer Allee 1. It has extensive exhibits of artefacts of the prehistoric, Roman and early Christian eras, including the original of the Roman wine boat from Neumagen.

The **Dom- und Diözesanmuseum** (Cathedral and Bishop's Museum) not far from the cathedral and Liebfrauenkirche, illustrates early Christian periods and sacred art. Among them are the ceiling paintings from the Constantine era (one of the subjects being probably a lady of the Imperial family) that were recovered from the Roman Imperial palace building that lies beneath the cathedral.

The **Simeonstift Municipal Museum** specialises in art and cultural artefacts from Trier's history up to the twentieth century and includes furniture, handicraft and folklore items. There is a three-storey **Toy Museum** in Nagelstrasse.

THE TRIER WINE TRADE

An important element in the economy of Trier is as a major centre for the wine trade, not only for its own immediate neighbourhood but for the whole Mosel valley. The most important wine estates and wine producers — such as the von Kesselstatts already mentioned and bodies such as the foundation which supports the 430-year old Friedrich Wilhelm Gymnasium (equivalent to a British grammar

The remarkable Roman monument at Igel

The attractive town of Bitburg in the Eifel

school) in Trier (Karl Marx was a former pupil) — derive their income not from a single great vineyard but from very many plots. These parcels of land are in the choicest sites of the most distinguished vineyards throughout the valley and have been acquired over centuries. The tourist information office can provide a considerable list of places in Trier where wines, not just from the immediate vicinity but from most of the notable Mosel villages, can be sampled. The city has a 3km (2 mile) long *Weinlehrpfad,* or wine instruction trail, around the hill called the Petrisberg. The trail starts just above the Amphitheatre, and with thirty-five stations it sets out explanations of the different grape varieties from which the wines are made, how they are cultivated, planted and tended throughout the year. In the wine-producing suburb of Olewig you can participate in cellar visits and tastings, and literature is available from the tourist information office at the Porta Nigra.

Excursions from Trier

Mention has been made of the popular seasonal boat excursion from Zurlauben to **Pfalzel**, 7km (4 miles) downstream, the summer residence of Roman emperors and Prince-Electors of Trier.

Another local excursion destination, only 8km (5 miles) to the south-west on the B53 (on the way to the Luxembourg frontier), is the village of **Igel** where there is a remarkable monument that has been described as the 'most handsome pagan monument north of the Alps'. The tall Igeler Säule, or Igel Column, is a 23m (75ft) high sculptured monumental pillar erected and touchingly inscribed to the memory of a wealthy Roman merchant family of cloth makers named Secundinius, who settled and made their home here in Gaul. It dates from about the year 250AD and its carvings document the prosperity of that era.

The Romans did not only leave behind artefacts and building structures, they also influenced the landscape. The increased population and prosperity required improved and extended agriculture. Many extensive villa sites have been uncovered in the region, including the type identified as the *villa rustica* that combined surroundings of gracious living with productive horticulture and farming — and of course viticulture. One example makes an interesting excursion from Trier. Take the road B51 — on the line of the old Roman road to Köln for 28km (17 miles) to **Bitburg** in the Eifel. Bitburg itself was a Roman military post and still has a section of Roman wall to show. As a change from wine Bitburg is a bonus for those who prefer beer; the quality of Bitburger Pils, which is famed far beyond its own province, is attributed to its excellent water sources. Take the B51a from Bitburg to Nattenheim (6km, 4 miles) and then the minor road east signposted to Fliessem for the **Villa Otrang**; this was the 'manor house' of a considerable Roman estate built in the first century AD and destroyed by Frankish invaders three centuries later. Last century's excavations revealed sixty-six rooms, hypocaust ducted heating structures, three bath houses and four magnificently coloured mosaic floors, forming one of the best-preserved Roman estate villas north of the Alps.

But perhaps best known of the Roman villas is that at **Nennig**, 32km (20 miles) upstream on the Mosel's east bank (opposite Remich in Luxembourg) which has the largest and best-preserved Roman mosaic floor north of the Alps with gripping pictorial scenes of gladiatorial combat.

For excursions further afield by private transport the variety is bewildering. Trier sits at the centre of a web of roads leading into areas described in this book: the Mosel, Rhine, Eifel and Hunsrück. Nor should one lose sight of the fact that Trier is a frontier city, with the Grand Duchy of Luxembourg only 10km (6 miles) away, and Luxembourg City only 44km, 28 miles.

Alternative Routes to the Mosel

With the advent of the European railway system English-speaking visitors travelled to the Mosel from the Channel ports by way of Brussels-Aachen-Köln-Koblenz. Even after the development of good roads many motorists prefered to arrive at the Mosel via the Rhine. This has tended to persist even though World War II demonstrated that motorised vehicles — even tanks — were not obliged to stick to the plains, but could penetrate hilly landscapes with fair ease. For those who wish to travel directly to the Mosel valley without necessarily going via the Rhine, one or two alternative approaches are worth considering and have merits of their own.

1 • FROM THE CHANNEL COAST TO TRIER VIA THE ARDENNES AND LUXEMBOURG

From Ostend or Zeebrugge on the Channel coast by way of Aalst, Brussels, Namur, the Belgian Ardennes to Bastogne, thence to Luxembourg and Trier.

2 • TO THE MIDDLE MOSEL VIA THE EIFEL

This route avoids Köln and the roads with heavy industrial traffic to its immediate west, and gives a fair sample of the landscape and small towns typical of the Eifel, while heading cross country direct to the Middle Mosel rather than the Rhine. This can be done in a single day's journey if the driver starts fresh in the morning after an overnight sleep on a ferry to Zeebrugge in Belgium or Europoort (south of Rotterdam) in Holland. From the coast head for just north of Liege ('Luik' in Dutch and 'Lüttich' on German road signs). This can be done using mainly motorways: from Zeebrugge by Belgian motor-roads A10 and A3, by-passing Brussels; from Europoort by the Dutch A1, by-passing Breda and Antwerp to continue on the A13 and then A3; the A3 passes to the north of Liege in either case.

Once past Liege continue on the A3 (now heading for the southern fringes of Aachen) until exit No 38 to Eupen. There turn south on road N67, through Eupen town (frontier adjustments were made in this area after World War I, before which Eupen had been German). After passing through unspoiled landscape into the heights of the Forest of Eupen for some 18km (11 miles) this hill road N67 (which is currently not particularly well surfaced) finally crosses the Belgian-German frontier near Mützenich and approaches the picturesque town of **Monschau**, very popular with German tourists. A fine panoramic view can be had 2km ($1^1/_4$ miles) short of the town from a signposted roadside viewpoint.

Monschau's old half-timbered houses are dovetailed into the narrow, steep-sided valley of the Rur and ranged at a variety of terrace levels on the hillsides. They present quite a colourful picture in pastel shades with their grey slate roofs merging into the background of forest greens. High above the town a medieval castle keep from the twelfth and fourteenth centuries looks down on the houses. Monschau stands almost in the centre of the German-Belgian Nature Park. Apart from the vernacular style half-timbered houses in Kirchstrasse and Holzmarkt, streets that go back to the end of the Thirty-Years' War, there is the old town hall of 1654 and also the baroque Rotes Haus, a wealthy cloth-maker's residence and office of 1760. Today it is an interesting museum illustrating eighteenth-century aristocratic life-style in the prosperous woollen cloth and silk manufacture which was based on the Eifel's water power. The castle above the town (part of which is now a youth hostel) goes back to the thirteenth and fourteenth centuries. The Eselturm (Asses' Tower) gives a fine view down to the town below.

Monschau is surrounded by a ring of satellite villages, which average about 5km (3 miles) away. These show interesting examples of the imposing house-high immaculately trimmed beech hedges that are grown round dwellings and farms here as a defence against the icy blasts of the prevailing winds from the High Eifel.

About 10km (6 miles) south of Monschau (near the Belgian border again) road B258 turns east to reach the climatic resort of **Schleiden** in the midst of hill and forest country. It too has a ruined keep. Its parish church has lovely stained glass windows from 1535. The town was the birthplace of the founder of Strasbourg University, Johannes Sturm. From Schleiden the wintersports villages in the Hohes Venn area are not far away.

From Schleiden the road runs south-east for 20km (12 miles) to Blankenheim. About half way it intersects a minor road which on the left leads to **Steinfeld** where there is a Premonstratensian Abbey founded around 1142. The abbey church is known locally as the Eifeldom, or Cathedral of the Eifel, where each year great music festivals take place. With its two round towers and massive structure it is almost like a fortress church.

Monschau in the North Eifel is a popular tourist destination

Blankenheim is another health resort and also a wintersports centre in the North Eifel. It is an attractive little town, with the twelfth-century castle of the Counts of Blankenheim enhancing the scene. This is another castle which plays a modern role as a romantically sited youth hostel. The town has two town gate-towers and also rampart walks. At its centre is an early eighteenth-century well house amid the half-timbered houses, where four springs rise which are the source of the river Ahr. Now road B258 follows the winding course of the Ahr's headwaters through charming rural scenery as far as the village of Musch, where the river turns north-east in the direction of Altenahr and Ahrweiler. Road B258 continues in a roughly easterly direction through the impressive forest scenery of the High Eifel to an important crossroads where it intersects the B257 from Adenau. At that intersection (unless you are tempted to visit the nearby famed Nürburgring motor racing track) turn right to follow the B257 south for 18km (11 miles) to the Ulmen junction with the A1/48, the Koblenz-Trier *Autobahn*.

From Ulmen there is quite a choice of routes to the Mosel valley. You can cross the *Autobahn* and continue south-east on B259 for 23km (14 miles) to reach the Mosel a short distance upstream from Cochem; or you can turn right, join *Autobahn* A1/48 south-west to Trier; or, turning right on to the *Autobahn*, you can travel just to the Wittlich exit (33km, 20 miles) from which you take road B50 south-east for 8km (5 miles) to reach the Mosel bridge at Zeltingen on the Mittelmosel between Traben-Trarbach and Bernkastel-Kues.

Routes to the Rhine from Trier and the Mosel

Visitors who have travelled upstream to Trier by car on the meandering but fascinating Mosel side roads may prefer, if returning to the Rhine, to take another route. A fast return to Koblenz can be made over the south-eastern edge of the Eifel by taking *Autobahn* A1/48 (which is also known by its European road number E44).

But a complete change of atmosphere can be enjoyed by taking the very good highway from Trier across the Hunsrück (south-east of the Mosel), known as the *Hunsrückhöhenstrasse*. Leave Trier south by road B268 via the suburb of Feyer and, passing through Pellingen, reach **Zerf** in 21km (13 miles), joining the B407, the *Hunsrückhöhenstrasse*, shortly before entering Zerf and crossing the river Ruwer. For some 27km (17 miles) the road has the Osburger Hochwald on the left and the Schwarzwalder Hochwald on the right. The Saarland frontier is not far away on the right (to the south) and is marked by the prominent height of the Teufelskopf, or Devil's Head. Crossing road B52 and shortly by-passing Hermeskeil, the *Höhenstrasse* is now numbered B327 and skirts the upper valley of the Dhron stream, passing close by Dhronecken and then **Thalfang**, where the little town is dominated by an attractive medieval church. Just beyond Thalfang the B327 is joined on the left by a scenic road that comes up from the river Dhron and Neumagen on the Mosel.

Morbach lies 10km (6 miles) further on, where roads come in from Idar-Oberstein on the south and from Bernkastel-Kues on the Mosel. The road continues to be very picturesque, passing through both high woodland and grazing country. In 16km (10 miles) beyond Morbach is a major road fork. To the right the B52 goes to Kirchberg (15km, 9 miles), and Simmern (24km, 15 miles). Simmern is the chief town of the Hunsrück, and Schloss Simmern houses the Hunsrück Museum and Archives. From Simmern there are minor roads that lead down steeply from the Hunsrück plateau to the towns and villages of the Rhine Gorge, such as Bacharach. But B327 continues to Kappel (13km, 8 miles) and **Kastellaun**. The ruins of Burg Kastellaun stand on an impressive rock shoulder above the town. It existed there in the early thirteenth century, but was among the first to be destroyed by Louis XIV's forces in 1689, and now provides visitors with a splendid viewpoint over the Hunsrück. From Kastellaun the Hunsrück road runs down to Koblenz (44km, 27 miles) by way of Emmelshausen and Buchholz, a hill suburb of Boppard on the Rhine.

Additional Information

Places of Interest

Alf
Burg Arras
Approach from road in Alf valley
Open: mid-March to mid-November.

Alken
Burg Thurant
☎ 02605 2004
Open: daily 8.30am-7pm
Wine museum, game-room museum, dungeon.

Bernkastel-Kues
St Nikolaus-Hospital
Cusanusstrasse 1
Open: mid-April to October, daily 10am-5pm; November-April 2-5pm.
Library and Moselweinmuseum.

Cusanus Birthplace
Nikolausufer 49
Open: mid-April to October, Tuesday-Saturday 10am-12noon, 2.30-5pm.
Documents, art.

Heimatmuseum 'Graacher Tor'
Open: Tuesday, Thursday, Friday 3-5pm, Saturday, Sunday 11am-12noon, 3-5pm.

Bitburg
Roman Villa
Otrang
Open: daily except Monday.

Enkirch
Heimatstuben-Museum
☎ 06541 9265

Open: during season Friday 6-7pm, Sat 5-7pm, Sunday 10am-12noon. Local museum with history, lifestyle and wine.

Idar-Oberstein
Deutsches Edelsteinmuseum (Precious Stone Museum) Diamond and Gem Exchange
☎ 06781 4821
Open: May-September daily 9am-6pm, October-May daily 9am-5pm.

Heimatmuseum
Hauptstr 436
☎ 06781 24619
Open: daily 9am-5.50pm.
Local history and gem industry.

Monschau
Rotes Haus
Open: Good Friday to November, tours at 10, 11am, 2, 3, 4pm daily (except Monday).

Moselkern
Burg Eltz
☎ 02762 1300
Open: April to October weekdays 9am-5.30pm, Sunday and holidays 10am-5.30pm.

Traben-Trarbach
Mittelmosel Museum
Ecke Mosel-str
☎ 06541 9480
Open: Tuesday to Sunday, telephone for times.
History, winelore.

Ikonenzentrum (Icon centre)
Graacherstr
Kautenbach
☎ 06541 3539
Open: Wednesday, Saturday, Sunday 2.30-5pm.

Trier
Landesmuseum
Weimarer Allee 1
Open: Monday to Friday 9.30am-4pm, Saturday 9.30am-1pm, Sunday 9am-1pm.
Entry fee, cafeteria.

Dom-Museum
Wind-str 6-7
Open: Monday to Saturday 9am-1pm, 2-5pm; Sunday 1-5pm.

Städtisches Museum
Simeonstift
Open: Tuesday to Friday 9am-5pm, Saturday, Sunday and holidays 10-1pm, closed Monday.

Karl-Marx-Haus
Brückenstrasse 10
Open: Monday 1-5pm; Tuesday to Sunday 10am-6pm.

Toy Museum
Nagelstrasse 4-5
Open: daily 10am-6pm.

Hotels

Bernkastel-Kues
Römischer Kaiser
Markt 29
☎ 06531 3038
Also restaurant

Mosel-blümchen
Schwanenstr 10
☎ 06531 2335
Good example of hotel family-run jointly with butcher's shop.

Hotel-Pension Graacher Tor
Graacherstr 22
☎ 06531 2566

Cochem
Alte Thorschenke
Brückenstr 3
☎ 02671 7059
Also restaurant. Fine cuisine.

Idar-Oberstein
Hotel zum Schwan
Hauptstr 25
☎ 06781 43081
Also restaurant.

Monschau
Hotel Burgau
St Vitherstr 16
☎ 02472 2545
Only evening meals for guests.

Traben-Trarbach
Altes Gasthaus Moseltor
Moselstr 1
☎ 6551
On the Trarbach side, not far from
river. Also restaurant.

Krone
An der Mosel 93
☎ 06541 6363
Also restaurant. Quiet site by river
on Traben side.

Trier
Hotel Eurener Hof
Eurenerstr 171
☎ 0651 88077
West-end hotel, large but family-
run. Also restaurant.

Hotel Petrisberg
Sickingenstr 11
☎ 0651 41181
On vineyard hill overlooking city.

Zell
Hotel zur Post
Schlossstr 21
☎ 06542 4217
Also restaurant.

Zeltingen
Nicolay zur Post
Uferallee 7
☎ 06532 2091
Fastidiously conducted and family
run. Also restaurant.

Restaurants

Bernkastel-Kues
Bernkasteler Ratskeller
Am Markt 30
☎ 06531 2204

Trier
Pfeffermühle
Zurlaubener Ufer 76
☎ 0651 41333

Tourist Information Offices

Bernkastel-Kues
Am Gestade 5
D5550 Bernkastel-Kues
☎ 06531 4023

Cochem
Endertplatz
D-5590 Cochem
☎ 02671 3971

Idar-Oberstein
Im Nahe-Center am Bahnhof
D-6580 Idar-Oberstein
☎ 06781 27025

Monschau
Stadtstrasse 1
Postfach 80
D-5108 Monschau
☎ 02472 33 00

Traben-Trarbach
Bahnstrasse 22
D5580 Traben-Trarbach
☎ 06541 90 11

Trier
An der Porta Nigra
Postfach 3830
D-5500 Trier
☎ 0651 48071

4
KOBLENZ TO BINGEN

If from Koblenz you resume an upstream river-cruise the first
features to catch the eye are Burg Lahneck above Oberlahnstein on
the east bank and Schloss Stolzenfels on the west, both of which have
already been described. If you do the journey by road this can be on
either side of the river, although most might prefer the west bank
route. By train, the west bank route from Koblenz is also more
spectacular. (German Rail Timetable 600.)

Almost facing Oberlahnstein, about 9km ($5^1/_2$ miles) upstream
from Koblenz on the west bank is the quaint little wine town of
Rhens, with its picturesque riverfront. It still has fair stretches of its
town fortifications, some fine half-timbered buildings including a
late gothic town hall as well as particularly lovely seventeenth- and
eighteenth-century mansions. Its fortifications are an indication that
for many centuries it had an importance that is belied by its modern
size. The boundaries of four of Germany's great Electoral Principali-
ties, those of Köln, Mainz, Trier and the Pfalz (Palatinate) met here.
And it was here that the seven Prince Electors took the oath of loyalty
to the medieval German emperors before their coronation in Aachen.
On a hill north of the town stands a stone monument known as the
✳ Königsstuhl (King's Seat). The original Königsstuhl went back to the
fourteenth century, was demolished by French invaders in 1803, but
was re-erected later in the nineteenth century. Still later it was moved
to the hilltop, where it now gives a good viewpoint.

On the opposite shore only a short distance upstream is **Braubach**,
another very attractive little town, thanks partly to the sense of unity
and shape given to it by the well-preserved surviving parts of its
fortifications, especially the Obertor or Upper Gate. Braubach is also
famed for rose growing, with a rose festival in June.

Standing on a 170m (558ft) crag above Braubach and serving as a landmark is Marksburg, one of the most handsome German castles and the only Middle Rhine hilltop fortress to escape destruction. It dates back to the twelfth/fourteenth centuries, with seventeenth-century bastions. It is well worth the climb to experience so authentic a medieval fortress, including its inner buildings. Its site appears so impregnable that it even escaped siege during Louis XIV's invasion. Its central keep — set in a triangular courtyard — is 39m (128ft) high and is founded on a square base that was part of the original castle of about 1200. Since the beginning of the twentieth century it has belonged to the Deutsche Burgenvereinigung (German Castles Association) who have converted it into a museum of castles and the 'Age of Chivalry'; it has a unique medieval botanic garden, as well as gruesome exhibits of instruments of torture and publishment. The castle also has a library for specialist research into historical studies related to castles. It is a 5 minute drive by car from Braubach, whereas the footpath takes 25 minutes. On the way a visit can also be paid to the old parish church of St Martin, with its Romanesque nave, early Gothic choir and fourteenth-century wall paintings.

After Braubach is a long S-bend in the river. What was the west bank at Rhens gradually becomes the north bank for about 6km ($3^3/_4$ miles) before executing a huge loop in the opposing direction to become the south-west bank. Here, on a long hollow shelf stands the picturesque town of **Boppard**. This river loop — known as the Bopparder Hamm and famed for its Riesling vineyards on the slopes — is the Rhine's largest. Boppard is another town with a Celtic and Roman history; indeed it possesses some of the best preserved remains of a fourth-century Roman fortress in Germany — and the Hotel Römerburg (Romans' Castle) stands on its foundations. Archaeological finds give evidence that *Bodobrica*, as it was then called, enjoyed great prosperity in the first three centuries AD. But most emblematic of Boppard is Balduinsburg, with its threatening six-storeyed square keep. This was built in 1340 by the Trier Electoral Prince Balduin to consolidate his grip on what was earlier a free imperial city. There is now a small local museum in the castle. Right on the river front the keep, along with the mighty twin towers of the collegiate church of St Severus, sets the characteristic outline of the town. Among many buildings of great interest is the Carmelite church that was built in the early fourteenth century; it contains several art treasures. The waterfront promenade of Boppard, with its colourful gardens, is a fascinating place to stroll and survey the lively river traffic. Here the vessels heading upstream begin to feel more markedly the force of the current as the river bed becomes more constricted by steeper and more closely set banks. Likewise, begin-

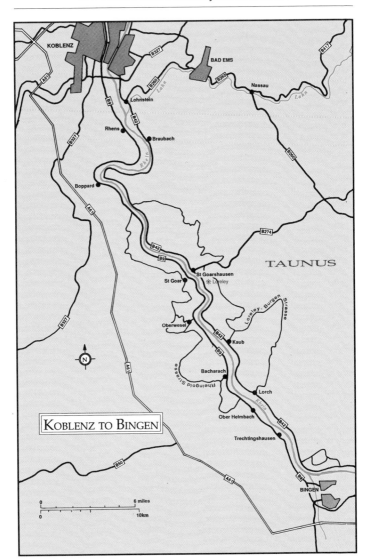

KOBLENZ TO BINGEN

ning with the Boppard Hamm, the main-line railway and river-side road are close together as they enter the Rhine gorge proper. This — and the Bopparder Hamm to the north — can be seen to great effect from the chairlift which runs up from the west of the town to a

The church of St Severus in the centre of Boppard

viewpoint known as the *Vierseenblick*, the View of Four Lakes, where the four glimpses of the river-loop seem to be of separate lakes.

Three kilometres (2 miles) upstream from Boppard, where the river is now flowing roughly south-north again, is the little spa of **Bad Salzig**, now part of the administrative district of Boppard. As its name suggests, its mineral waters are slightly saline. The spa establishments and parkland lie just to the west of the attractive little town. Here the otherwise narrow Middle Rhine valley widens into a hollow shelf behind which the hills rise fairly gently. It is particularly attractive at blossom time in spring, because this obviously fertile shelf supports cherry orchards that for two centuries have played an important part in the local economy.

Diagonally across the Rhine from Bad Salzig is the twin-town of **Kamp-Bornhofen**. River navigators regard this as marking the precise beginning of the Rhine gorge, whose walls are seen looming cliff-like ahead. On the rocky ridge above Kamp-Bornhofen are two castles not only within sight of one another but apparently confronting one another across a wall and moat. So they are known locally as the *'Feindliche Brüder'* (Hostile Brothers). Slightly lower than its neighbour on the ridge, Burg Sterrenberg was an imperial stronghold in the twelfth-century. It was abandoned in the mid-sixteenth century, became ruinous but was partially restored in the late twentieth century and is now administered by the State. Burg Liebenstein was built in the thirteenth-century and has a fourteenth-century residential tower of some importance. Both castles have an approach road, car park and restaurant and are open daily to the public. There is also a ridge footpath from Bornhofen (30 minutes).

The thousand-year old town of Bornhofen is a long-established place of pilgrimage on account of the Gothic church of 1435 which stands at the foot of the rocky ridge leading to the two castles. The town also has in its town hall an interesting Flösser- und Schiffer-Museum with exhibits illustrating the life and work of raftsmen and shipmen in the Rhine Gorge. A boat-excursion upstream can be taken to the famed Loreley. The little town is well-placed for excursions by road to the Loreley rock — and to the Lahn valley further north, as is also Braubach.

On the cliff-top 8km (5 miles) further upstream is the castle known generally as **Burg Maus**, 'Mouse Castle', which was built in the mid-fourteenth century to guard the interests of the Prince Archbishop of Trier. In its day it was considered to be one of the best fortified castles, and the archbishop himself used it as his residence for some time. Napoleon blew it up in 1806 along with other Rhineland fortifications, but it was restored to the original plans at the beginning of the twentieth century. It is open to visitors all year. A footpath takes 25 minutes from the little town of **Wellmich** (nowadays part of St Goarshausen district administration). Wellmich has a Gothic parish church of about the same date as the castle which is considered one of the most beautiful in the valley, with some fine frescoes.

At Burg Maus is an eagle and falcon aviary where demonstrations are given by free-flying eagles, falcons and kites against the dramatic background of the medieval castle and above the Rhine valley. The demonstrations are accompanied by a commentary.

Almost directly facing the Maus on the opposite side of the river, 115m (377ft) above it, is the ruin of the mightiest of all Rhine castles, **Burg Rheinfels**. Its main structure was started in 1245 for the Count von Katzenelnbogen, a very powerful magnate in this region, to help exact river-tolls. Ten years later it had to stand up to a very ferocious siege (arising from a revolt over an increase in tolls!) which lasted a year — yet failed to budge the count. In 1692 it was the only Rhineland fortress that withstood Louis XIV's artillery. Yet a century later it fell into the hands of French revolutionary forces and was ultimately blown up. In 1843 the Prince of Prussia purchased the ruins to save them. As the most comprehensive castle remains on the Rhine they are most instructive and in particular the medieval keep and the underground passages of the later fortress extensions are most impressive. So too is the museum. It is open to the public, guided tours are available, and there is a car park.

St Goar lies on the river below Burg Rheinfels, and is linked by a car-ferry with its twin across the river, **St Goarshausen**. As both towns have much of interest in them, it is a busy ferry; and though its crossing is a short one it too is not lacking in interest, for this stretch of the Rhine is busy with river traffic. Excursion ships, motorized barges and tankers, box-barges for bulk-cargo which are clamped together and pushed by a modern pusher-unit — all had room enough further downstream and will also have it further upstream. Here they are constrained by the gorge, and the force of the current is boosted for the same reason so that upstream traffic seems to be progressing slowly with great effort, while downstream vessels often appear to be travelling faster than their helmsmen find comfortable. Little wonder that the skippers of small yachts and pleasure craft welcome the chance of ducking into St Goar's little harbour for a respite before tackling the stream again. On St Goar's waterfront is the headquarters of the river pilotage and traffic control and a Rhine navigation signal-station.

First-time visitors to the gorge do not think it remarkable that express trains thunder through so frequently on the riverside rail-

The ruins of the massive Burg Rheinfels at St Goar

The Loreley rock, now in domesticated surroundings

Burg Katz looks down on St Goarshausen

way, yet they tend to be astonished by the bulk of the river traffic. Like the railway much of the river traffic is not local but international, not just the cruise vessels but also the tankers and bulk-carriers passing between Switzerland and Holland and places between.

The colourful twin-towns with the attractive promenade gardens both get their name from a hermit saint who lived here in the sixth century and whose little chapel became later the site of St Goar's one-time collegiate church and now the parish church in the town centre. Its beautiful eleventh-century crypt is known as the 'Saint's Vault' and was for long a place of pilgrimage. The network of little alleys with their wine bars, wine-growers', shipmen's and fishermen's houses is as vital, colourful and stimulating as the riverside.

St Goarshausen, across the river, was like its twin a small fortified town. It still has two towers remaining from the fourteenth-century town fortifications. The quaint houses at its romantic-looking old centre look as if they had been squeezed gently into the narrow space between the river and rock-face of the gorge. From the little town a road leads uphill and upstream to what is probably Germany's best known rock, the **Loreley**, a huge mass of slate, 132m (433ft) high, that bulges out narrowing still further the course of the river. Echoes caused by the huge rock are the probable explanation of the 'siren voices' which old legend says distracted helmsmen and caused disaster and drowning. River conditions were particularly danger-ous before engineers used explosives to deal with some of the reefs and rapids in these narrows. Even today the channel's width here is only about 100m (330ft), compared to more than 800m (2,625ft) at Rüdesheim barely 30km (18 miles) upstream. On the larger passen-ger ships a band or loudspeaker, the odd musician or a group of voices will be sure to strike up the plaintive melody that accompa-nies the words of Heinrich Heine's sad romantic poem of the Loreley siren-maiden and the shipman — now so well-known that this Middle Rhine district is widely known as the 'Loreley Valley'.

Nowadays the plateau that lies above the Loreley is used as an amphitheatre accommodating some 10,000 spectators for folklore events and open-air festivals during the high season. On the cliff top is also a hotel-restaurant and a youth hostel.

But towering above St Goarshausen on a splendid protruding rock-site is another castle, erected in 1371 by the von Katzenelnbogen family that had already built Rheinfels across the river. Its main purpose was to co-operate with Rheinfels in levying river-tolls as from it there is an early sight of vessels navigating the Loreley rock. The castle's full name was Neu-Katzenelnbogen but is generally shortened (not surprisingly) to Burg Katz. (As *Katz* is German for 'cat' there is an obvious play on its relationship with Burg Maus only 2km ($1^1/_4$ miles) away on the same hill-top!) It was blown up in 1806, rebuilt at the end of the century and since has had various modern extensions. It now houses a convalescent home, so can only be visited by special arrangement.

Back on the west bank, 6km ($3^3/_4$ miles) further upstream from St Goar lies **Oberwesel**, another town with a Celtic and a Roman past. Also a former imperial free city (that once issued its own coinage), it preserves much of its heritage. It was the most strongly fortified town of the Middle Rhine; the old city wall had sixteen watchtowers, although some are now ruinous but others well preserved. This town of winegrowers and shipmen extends along an attractive riverfront with the picturesque background of castle Schönburg poised on the edge of a steep cliff, its curtain-wall presenting an impressive picture of medieval military competence. At the north end of the town the same note is struck by the most impressive of the surviving city-towers, the massive round fourteenth-century Ochsenturm (Ox's Tower) — nowadays lighted to serve as a beacon for the river traffic. Not far from it the old parish church of St Martin also has a fortress air with its stout tower from the early fourteenth century crowned with battlements; in contrast its interior contains valuable works of art. So too does the town's other collegiate church, the beautiful *Liebfrauenkirche* (Church of Our Lady) — commonly described from its sandstone as *die Rote Kirche*, the Red Church.

The impressive Schönburg castle is first referred to in 1149; a century later the Schönburg family, whose wealth came from river toll, greatly extended it. Destroyed in 1689 the castle was restored two centuries later. Today it is partly an international youth hostel, as well as a castle-hotel with a restaurant.

Heading upstream on the river from here, strangers are often taken aback with what appears ahead (especially if it is hazy) to be the sight of a large warship confronting them. This phenomenon is the *Pfalzgrafenstein* (Count Palatine's Rock) generally called *die Pfalz*. This is a little fortress occupying with great neatness a rocky island in the river almost opposite the east-bank village of Kaub. It was built in 1327 for the purpose once again of simplifying the exaction of tolls, in this case by King Ludwig the Bavarian. It was extended in the early seventeenth century and in more recent times has served as a convenient signal station for river traffic. It is extremely picturesque from almost any angle. It can be visited by motor-boat from Kaub ferry stage and is an excursion destination from Oberwesel.

Kaub itself, about 4km ($2^1/_2$ miles) upstream from Oberwesel, is another little place with well-preserved medieval walls. Three of the fortification's towers, connected by an arcade, together with the tollhouse and the sixteenth-century courthouse give the place a picturesque appearance. As the position of the Pfalz would suggest, Kaub was an important point for the collection of tolls from passing vessels. For the same reason shipmen from Kaub regularly manned the pilotage service on the river. Apart from being a wine village it was also a distribution point for the slate trade. It has two very picturesque and romantic streets, Auf der Mauer and Metzgergasse. At the turn of the year 1813-14 the Prussian Field Marshal Blücher chose Kaub as the place to take his army across the Rhine in pursuit of French armies in the final campaign of the Napoleonic wars. This is commemorated by the Blücher Memorial on the Rhine Promenade with the castle of Gutenfels high above and the Kaub vineyards in the mid-ground providing a fitting back-drop. There is also a Blücher Museum in his one-time quarters in the Metzgergasse,

Burg Gutenfels was built at the beginning of the thirteenth century. Its main features — a 35m (114ft) high keep and a four-sided main building — are well preserved. For a long period during the Thirty Years' War it was the headquarters of Gustav Adolf of Sweden. After demolitions in the Napoleonic era it was later skilfully restored and nowadays it is appreciated for its style and spacious lay-out and is a hotel. It has a 3km (2 mile) approach road from Kaub.

Bacharach lies 7km (4$^1/_2$ miles) along road B9 from Oberwesel. It too has preserved its circuit of fourteenth/sixteenth-century town walls; and the roofed sentry walk along the walls on the riverfront makes an interesting introductory stroll. The town's income from river tolls and its wine trade made it a wealthy place. In the Middle Ages it was the main trading centre, warehousing depot and river port for the wines, not only from the Middle Rhine, but also from the Nahe and the famed Rheingau vineyards stretching between Rüdesheim and Hochheim. In those days only boats of very small size could slip through the hazardous barrier reefs of the notorious Binger Loch that lay in the Rhine upstream. Bacharach therefore became a transhipment harbour for the valuable wine trade. Its walls and buildings reflect this importance, and its annual wine markets led to the development of cattle markets and other trading outlets.

It became a possession of the Count Palatine in the eleventh century. Its sturdy Peterskirche (church of St Peter) goes back to the same period, and has a lovely interior with valuable frescoes. Its Romanesque west-tower is reminiscent of St Martin's in Oberwesel. In contrast is the delicacy of the elegant ruin of the Wernerkapelle's unfinished Gothic building among the vineyards. In the town itself are attractive historic inns and wine bars; picturesque houses at and

The Pfalz, built on an island in the middle of the Rhine at Kaub

The attractive half-timbered Altes Haus in Bacharach, built in 1568

near the Market Place include the fourteenth-century Altes Haus which is one of the Rhine's most famed half-timbered houses, the adjacent Grüner Baum (Green Tree) and Alte Münze (Old Mint) facing the latter, all three being wine bars of note. The Old Mint derives its name from the fact that between 1386 and 1465 the coinage of the Palatinate realm was minted in this fascinating old half-timbered building.

The line of the old town defensive walls turns uphill to link with the fortifications of the Count Palatine's castle in this region, Burg Stahleck. Town and castle shared stirring times during the merciless Thirty Years' War. The castle was destroyed by the French in 1689, and rebuilt in exemplary style as a youth hostel in the present century. It is reached by a 10-minute climb from the town. A particularly attractive path leads to it from the picturesque corner where a surviving section of the town-wall ramparts and the Steeger Tor (city-gate leading to the satellite wine village of Steeg) meets the steep vineyard slopes.

The valley road to Steeg continues to climb in corkscrew bends on to the Hunsrück high plateau at Rheinböllen and then on to the Hunsrück 'county town' of Simmern — a pleasant excursion.

The Middle Rhine towns vie with each other in the lay-out of their spacious parks and gardens on the Rhine front. And Bacharach is no exception. Its Rhine front garden/park leads upstream to a pleasant camping site with a nearby sandy beach which has built up where the full force of the Rhine has concentrated towards the opposite shore.

A few kilometres upstream but on the other, east, bank is the long-established wine-town of **Lorch** at the valley-mouth of the tributary river Wisper. It owed its prosperity in the early medieval period to being the downstream station of a portage known as the *Kaufmanns Weg* (Merchants' Road) which used the Wisper valley as part of a route for the transhipment of goods over the Rheingau hills to Rüdesheim to avoid both the navigational hazards of the next section of the Rhine and the payment of hefty tolls on the river.

Lorch's great treasure is its finely proportioned St Martinskirche in the Market Place on its terrace above the Rhine. The church furnishings, particularly the magnificent fifteenth-century high altar triptych with niches for ten statues is one of the priceless artistic masterpieces of Middle Rhine art. The choir stalls, carved with medieval animal motifs, are contemporary with the late thirtenth-century foundation of the church itself. The five-story Hilchen-haus with its imposing gable-façade is a Renaissance residence that dominates the river. There is also a gothic tithe-barn and a number of more modest but charming half-timbered houses in the picturesque, crooked lanes and alleys behind. For those not sated with Rhine valley castles, from Lorch a short excursion up the Wisper valley in the direction of the Taunus hills reveals several imposing ruins such as Geroldstein. A short distance into the valley stands a baroque seventeenth-century pilgrimage church, the Heiligkreuzkapelle.

Diagonally facing Lorch across the river (back on road B9) is the straggling village of **Niederheimbach**. When the scheduled passenger excursion ship puts into the landing-stage here, families with young children regularly disembark. On a rock-shelf about 30m (100ft) above the village is *Märchenhain* or 'Fairytale Grove' where in a charming landscape favourites from the rich repertory of German fairy-tales and legends are represented life-size in stone.

Niederheimbach has something of interest for adults in the form of an extensive *Weinlehrpfad* (wine instruction trail) with several types and varieties of grapevine displayed and explained, so providing an informative walk of some 2km (1$^1/_4$ miles) up the idyllic valley to the wine village of Oberheimbach.

Only 4km (2$^1/_2$ miles) from Niederheimbach is the old wine village of **Trechtingshausen**. Between Niederheimbach and Trechtingshausen is Burg Sooneck, most readily accessible from Niederheimbach by a 2km (1$^1/_4$ miles) carriage-way and then on a 1km ($^2/_3$ mile) footpath. The castle stands in very picturesque surroundings on a prominence that is really an outrider of the Hunsrück's Soon Forest (pronounced as English 'zone'). It is thought to be of eleventh-century date, suffered several destructions but was restored when inherited by Prussia's Crown Prince in 1834. Its nucleus is a fourteenth-century keep which today is noteworthy for its collection of armour and equipment from the age of chivalry along with historic furniture. It can be visited any day except Monday, and refreshments are available.

Not far away, above Trechtingshausen, is another castle which had an infamous reputation in early medieval times as a *Raubritter's* (robber-baron's) nest. Indeed in 1282 Burg Reichenstein (or Falkenburg, its other name) was destroyed and its *Raubritter* executed by King Rudolf of Hapsburg for despoiling travellers. Nowadays it is one of Germany's castle hotels. Its museum has a fine collection of weaponry, hunting-trophies, and period furniture.

Only 2km (2$^1/_4$ mile) south of Trechtinghausen is the third of a remarkable trio of castles in this district. Burg Rheinstein, on its crag overhanging road B9, is perhaps even better known than its well known neighbours as it was among the very first of the castles reconstructed under the influence of nineteenth-century Rhine romanticism. Probably of thirteenth-century foundation, its ruin was

River Traffic

The Rhine has one of the highest concentrations of river traffic in the world. Not only is it used by passenger vessels, but every day millions of tons of goods are transported on it in both directions. It is an international waterway, so German, Swiss, French and Dutch river vessels carry bulk cargoes such as oil, metallic ores, coal, grain, gravel and sand, which can be moved more economically and conveniently by water than by land. Many of these cargoes are conveyed on self-propelled motor barges. Many more are conveyed on vessels that have no power units themselves. Not many years ago lines of these, tied head to tail, used to be towed by tugs. Nowadays the tugs have been replaced by pusher units. These are in effect floating platforms with very powerful machinery for driving mighty propellors. Their squat bows are reinforced by huge buffers, and in front of them are clamped 'box-barges' loaded with bulk cargoes. These they push — instead of towing as the tugs did. This has several advantages: the clamped box-barges take up less river space than barge-lines under tow, and they are under firmer control in the current.

The pusher units have a very lofty superstructure which carries the navigation bridge right forward in their bows. This high position enables the master not only to see clearly ahead of his barges, but also to see further round the next bend on river loops.

With all this heavy traffic, there are strict 'rules of the road', although it might appear to the uninitiated that international navigation rules are being flouted. There are special considerations on rivers that require the general rules to be overridden, the most common being the force of the river's current. So, for instance, vessels travelling downstream have priority over those travelling upstream as it is much more difficult to stop a ship going with the current than one pushing against it. Also a ship's rudder has not so much 'grip' on the water when the current is possibly near to overtaking the ship, so steering is more difficult when proceeding downstream.

acquired by Prince Friedrich Ludwig of Prussia in 1823. He was responsible for reconstructing the little medieval keep into a princely summer residence in romantic style. In the last quarter of the twentieth century it was purchased by a distinguished German opera singer who restored it and has given it a new lease of life as one of the major attractions of this area with its romantic turrets and terraces.

When two ships are on a collision course the rule of the sea is that they avoid each other by each keeping to starboard (right-hand). Sometimes however in a river that could be difficult or impossible — if for instance the captain of a heavily-laden vessel knows that the water depth to starboard is insufficient for his draught. In such a case he gives the other captain advance warning that he intends to pass on the other side. This is done by a blue flag pushed out very conspicuously from the bridge towards the side on which he intends to pass. Nowadays on modern vessels the blue flag is replaced by a blue shutter-panel that can be operated swiftly by electrical or mechanical control, or a flashing light at night. A ship also gives others notice of her intentions by sounding a siren or whistle: a single sharp short blast means 'I am altering course to star-board' (right), two sharp short blasts indicates 'port' (left), and three means the intention is to reverse.

A freighter dispays the blue signal to starboard to indicate that he intends to hold course to port

The interior decoration and fine furniture are an added attraction.

Almost opposite, on the east bank is **Assmannshausen** $7^1/_2$ km, ($4^1/_2$ miles) from Lorch on road B42. This is a very familiar name to those who favour the best German red wines, for which this wine town has been famed since the eleventh-century. Its vineyards are reputed to have been planted a thousand years earlier even than that.

Its hostelries throng the Rhine front — many were the haunts of young Rhineland poets and musicians of the nineteenth-century Romantic movement. Today a popular resort, it is now incorporated in the administrative district of Rüdesheim (out of sight upstream because of the right-angled turn taken by the Rhine in between). Assmannshausen, itself surrounded with vineyards, lies at the foot of the wooded hills of the Niederwald. From it a cable car ascends in fifteen minutes to the Niederwald forest where many well laid-out and marked rambling trails exist. One such leads to the Niederwald memorial, a statue on a high plinth of a female figure emblematic of Germania. This was erected in the nineteenth century as a memorial to the unification of Germany under Prussia and to the rebirth of a German Empire. Perhaps the most tactful way of commenting on the statue itself would be to accept the advice of a post-World War II German writer: 'Let's not spend too much time on what is, artistically, a really questionable work for our modern taste; rather let us enjoy the beautiful view here over the Rhine and its islands, upon Bingen over there and the lovely Nahe valley.' The same statue and viewpoint can be reached by another cable-railway, from Rüdesheim that lies round the big river bend.

But before Rüdesheim is reached, whether by road or by ship from Assmannshausen, the ruins of Ehrenfels come in sight, halfway up the hillside, amid the vineyards. Ehrenfels castle was another fortification set up specifically to make sure of gathering river tolls, this time by the Prince-Archbishop of the great city of Mainz further upstream. The great castle on the hill was backed up by a smaller fort on an island in the river. The combination could effectively blockade passage on the river, or collect passage-money, just as Schloss Gutenfels and Pfalz did at Kaub.

The toll station was well chosen, as this was always a dangerous stretch of river. Known as the Binger Loch, it derived its name from the large town of Bingen on the south-west shore — and the word *loch* meaning a 'gap'. For here is where the Rhine, after flowing broadly and quietly through its Rhine plain, first had to break through that great slate-rock mass of the Rhenish Schist Uplands. The break-through point is not only narrow, but also it has a river bed of jagged rock and is interspersed with reefs. On the reefs a little fort or *Maut-turm* (*maut* being an archaic word for 'toll') was built to collect tolls. For a very long time the little fort has been known as the *Mäuseturm* (Mice-Tower) and in best Rhineland tradition the legend is now told that it got its name because of an archbishop so cruel and so miserly that the poor mice, for whom there were no pickings in his castle, pursued him even when he fled to the little tower on the Rhine and there took vengeance by devouring him!

The tower fell into decay when toll exaction ended. But during the Romantic movement such was the popular nostalgia for it that in 1855 it was restored. It was used as a signal station for river-traffic control until 1974.

The Rhine is joined from the south by a sizeable tributary, the river Nahe, and the city of Bingen arose at the confluence just as Koblenz did at the mouth of the Mosel. Bingen on the south bank directly faces Rüdesheim on the north. From near Kaub the Rhine is the boundary between two German *Länder* or 'states', so that Bingen lies in Rheinland-Pfalz (most of the region covered by this book), while Assmannhaussen and Rüdesheim lie in the state of Hessen.

Rüdesheim, 7km ($4^1/_4$ miles) further on the B42 from Assmanns-hausen, has this century become one of the Middle Rhine's most popular resorts thanks to its attractive wines grown on south-facing slopes, the attractive scenery of the town and its forest hinterland, and the reputation of its townspeople for good humour, good cheer and hospitality. People who know no other German street names but Unter den Linden can remember the Drosselgasse as the street lined with pubs and wine taverns ringing with music, dance and song.

The town lies under the long line of the Niederwald hills sheltering from north winds the vineyards said to be planted during the reign of Charlemagne. Rüdesheim offers not only the enjoyment of local wines but also opportunities for some not-too-demanding education in the life-style and work of the *Winzer* who produce it. Excursions can be made to the premises of the wine trade and to those of the distillers of Germany's distinguished Asbach Uralt brandy. At the Asbach distillery there are regular tours with an English speaking guide, followed by a free tasting and, of course, an opportunity to buy their familiar products. The locally grown grapes are regarded as too high a quality for brandy and visitors are surprised to learn that grapes are imported from the Cognac region of France — the difference in taste from the French product being solely due to variations in the maturing process. ✳

Alleyways with charming half-timbered houses lead to the Ober-strasse where there are still some of the old aristocratic houses such as numbers 4 and 5. Also, at number 27 stands the Brömserhof with its richly painted interiors; the handsome late-gothic and renais-sance-style residence of the local Brömser family. In this manor house is now the Mechanisches Musikkabinett, a museum contain- 🏠 ing one of the largest collections of self-playing musical instruments from the past three centuries. The same family's even more striking fortified residence in Rhein-strasse, the thousand-year-old Brömserburg, was once a castle with the waters of the Rhine forming its moat. For centuries it was a residence of the Archbishop of Mainz. Today it is the home of the Rheingauer Heimat- und Wein-Museum, with among other things a valuable collection of drinking vessels. There is also a *Weinlehrpfad* in the town, which starts at the Ringmauer and stretches along Panoramaweg to finish at the Brömserburg Wine-museum. At the eastern end of Rheinstrasse is the 20m (65ft) high *Adlerturm* (Eagle Tower) that was formerly part of the town's defences on the very edge of the Rhine. From the pedestrian precinct of the Oberstrasse there is a cable-car to the Niederwald Monument, mentioned in connection with Assmannshausen.

Rüdesheim has an immense number of activities available from pony-riding to waterskiing. It is well-placed for excursions including to places of interest in the Rheingau area, which is considered to begin here and run to Mainz-am-Rhein (see Chapter 5).

The Mäuseturm, built on a reef in the Rhine near Bingen, with the ruins of Ehrenfels behind

The spirit stills at the Asbach distillery, Rüdesheim

Brömserburg at Rüdesheim now houses a museum of wine

From Trechtingshausen road B9 reaches **Bingen** in $6^1/_2$ (4 miles). Before crossing the river Nahe into the city proper, it passes through Bingerbrück, a suburb on the left bank of the river. Bingen differs from the other Middle Rhine towns by being in a very open situation at the mouth of the Nahe. This had both strategic and commercial importance, lying at a point where trade roads met and where the Rhine had navigation problems. The Romans recognised this and made a station here, but Bingen's open situation in times of invasion was a disadvantage. Little remains from its historic buildings. In the old town is the fine Gothic collegiate church of St Martin built from 1404 onwards which underwent late-Gothic development a century later. However it has an impressive crypt that is a relic of an original romanesque eleventh-century church that was burned down and replaced by the fifteenth-century building. From the Roman period survive the foundations of a fort upon which was later raised the Romanesque keep of Burg Klopp. This castle on a hill in the middle of the city was a possession of the Archbishop of Mainz; having suffered destruction like others in 1689 it was blown up in 1711, but rebuilt in the later nineteenth century. Now it houses the city's administration and an interesting folk museum. The museum has a unique exhibit: the comprehensive set of surprisingly varied surgical instruments of a Roman physician of the second century AD.

The Nahe Valley and Bad Kreuznach

An excursion from Bingen not to be missed, 15km (9 miles) south on road B48, is to **Bad Kreuznach** on the river Nahe. The spa town is surrounded by vineyards and with a hinterland featuring the Hunsrück's wooded hills in the triangle between the Rhine, Mosel and Saar. Its saline springs are reputed to have been used for bathing and for therapeutic drinking since pre-Roman times. Its treatment centres have all the up-to-date therapeutic aids as well as a range of the long-established facilities, including lovely, peaceful spa-parkland and almost all conceivable leisure activities. All the spa facilities are sited in an elegant district on an island, Badewörth, that is linked by the old Nahe bridge to the old town. Emblematic of Bad Kreuznach is a group of fascinating and picturesque bridge houses that have stood on two pillars of the historic stone bridge, with their half-timbered gables facing the stream, since the fifteenth century. The house on the seventh pillar still preserves, lodged in its façade, a cannon ball from a Swedish bombardment in 1632 during the Thirty Years' War. The bridge itself goes back to before 1300; half of it was blown up in 1945 and two of the original nine pillars lost. Even so it still ranks as a fine example of medieval civil engineering. Above the medieval churches of the *Altstadt* and the kaleidoscope of roofs of many surviving old-time houses rise the remains of the thirteenth-century Kauzenburg castle, which has survived the assaults of the Thirty Year' War but not the French of 1689; within its ruins is a modern restaurant — with a good view over the town.

Bad Kreuznach has two interesting museums: in the Castle Park there is a museum with geological, prehistoric and historical sections; while in the Römerhalle are finds from the Roman era, including the 'Gladiators' mosaic-floor with hypocaust heating (one of the finest mosaics anywhere north of the Alps), uncovered a century ago on the line of the Roman military road to Trier and Metz.

Public Transport Option: Bad Kreuznach has a good rail service from Bingerbrück (15-20 minutes journey), DB Timetable 650. Bingerbrück, like Bingen, lies on the main line rail service on the Rhine left-bank Köln-Koblenz-Mainz route (DB Timetable 600). On the opposite bank most places are served by the Koblenz-Rüdesheim-Wiesbaden service (DB Timetable 611). These railway journeys are among the most interesting in Europe, especially the left (ie west) bank line which clings closely to the river for most of the way, including the spectacular Rhine-loop at Boppard.

But to get to know the Rhine at leisure and to appreciate what is most interesting on both banks, a journey by ship is recommended. Even the leading German motorist's organisation advocates this to its members pointing out that if you travel the Rhine gorge by car, you will be consumed by envy of the ships passing peacefully on the river. A passenger ship takes $3^3/_4$ hours from Bingen to Koblenz; in the opposite direction, upstream, just over five hours. With an express service a little less.

For visitors with private transport it is only 6km ($3^3/_4$ miles) from Bad Kreuznach to **Bad Münster-am-Stein**, another spa town with warm-springs for therapeutic treatment but supplying also an open-air swimming pool. Its remarkable landscape draws many visitors. The little town is virtually shut in on three sides by rock-faces. One of them, the Rotenfels (Red Rock), is unique in Europe north of the Alps. This is an immense mass of porphyritic rock that towers vertically from the river, its face scored with fissures and crevices, an eerie sight mirrored in the gentle flow of the river. Scenic minor roads follow the Nahe upstream through the vineyards and wine-villages of the Nahe white-wine district to **Sobernheim**, (is another climatic resort catering for sufferers from rheumatic and metabolic disorders), then to **Kirn**, a little medieval town set in mixed woodlands at the lower slopes of the Hunsrück. The Hunsrück possesses the most extensive and lovely woodlands and forests in all Germany — and that is quite a claim. Eighteen kilometres (11 miles) from Kirn road 41 leads west along the river Nahe to the gem-working town of Idar-Oberstein (see Chapter 3).

Public Transport Option: The route just described can be done by rail from Bad Kreuznach to Idar Oberstein, via the places mentioned, in 40 to 50 minutes (DB Timetable 640).

Additional Information

Places of Interest

Bacharach
Burg Stahleck
Now youth hostel, reached by footpath (10 minutes)
Open: Apr-Sept 9am-1pm, 2-6pm; Oct-Mar 9am-1pm, 2-5pm. Closed Mondays and December

Bad Kreuznach
Schlossparkmuseum
Dessauerstr 49
Open: daily except Mon, 9am-12.30pm,2-6pm

Römerhalle (Gladiator-mosaic)
Huffelsheimerstr 5
Open: daily except Mon, 9am-12.30pm, 2-6pm

Bingen
Heimatmuseum
Burg Klopp
Open: April-mid October, Tues-Sun 9am-12 noon, 2-5pm, closed Mon.

Mäuseturm
On island near Bingerbrück
Visit by boat

Boppard
Museum der Stadt Boppard
Burgstrasse 2

Open: April-October, Tues-Fri 10am-12 noon, 2-5pm, Sat 10am-12noon, Sun 2-4pm, closed Mon.

Braubach
Marksburg
Museum of the German Castles Association
☎ 02627 206
Open: Easter to Oct, continuous admission 10am-5pm; Nov-Easter hourly, 11am-5pm.

Kamp-Bornhofen
Raft- and Ship-men's Museum
Rathaus
☎ 06773 360
Open: Wed 2.30-5.30pm and by arrangement

Burg Liebenstein
☎ 06773 308
Burg Sterrenberg
☎ 06773 323
Both have access road, car park and restaurant. Open daily but check by telephone

Kaub
Blüchermuseum
Metzgergasse 6
Open: daily except Tues, 10am-12noon, 2-4pm. Nov to end March 10am-12pm

Pfalz
Visited by motor-boat (if river levels are normal) March to Oct daily except Mon

Gutenfels Castle
(now hotel-restaurant)
☎ 06774 220

Niederheimbach
Burg Sooneek
☎ 06743 6064
2km access road, then 1km path
Open: daily except Monday and December, Apr-Sept 9am-1pm, 2-6pm, Oct-Mar 9am-1pm, 2-5pm

Oberwesel
Heimatmuseum
Rathausstr 6
Open: Tues & Thur 2-4.30pm.

Rüdesheim
Rheingau Museum and Museum of Wine History
Brömserburg, Rhein-strasse
Open: mid-March to mid-Nov daily 9am-6pm

Seilbahn Rüdesheim
Oberstrasse 37
Chairlift to Niederwald

Weinbrennerei Asbach
Rheinstrasse
Regular distillery tours with German or English speaking guide

Mechanisches Musikkabinett
(Museum of Musical Boxes)
Brömserhof
Oberstrasse 27

St Goar
Burg Rheinfels
(access by road)
Open: April-Oct daily

Heimatmuseum
Burg Rheinfels
Open March-Oct daily 9.30am-12noon, 1-5pm;

Puppenmuseum (Toy Museum)
Open: Tues-Sun 10am-12.30pm, 2-7pm. Mon 10am-12.30pm.

St Goarshausen
Burg Katz
Open only by request.

Burg Maus
☎ 06771 7669
Free-flying eagles, falcons etc.
Open: Easter-Sept 10am-6pm daily, flights with commentary at 11.00am, 2.30pm, 4.30pm

Trechtingshausen
Burg Rheinstein
☎ 06721 6377
Open: Mar-Nov 9am-7pm
Has restaurant

Schloss Reichenstein
☎ 06721 6101
Open: mid-Mar to mid-Nov 9am-6pm
Castle hotel with museum

Hotels and Restaurants

Bacharach
Altkölnischer Hof
Bluecherstr 2
☎ 06743 1339
Typical Rhinelander style

Hotel Pension (Garni)
Malerwinkel
Blücherstr 41
In quiet picturesque corner of old town walls.

Park-Café
Markt 8
☎ 06743 1422.

Bacharach-Steeg
Hotel Restaurant beim Schlemmer
  Paul
Blücherstr 159
☎ 06743 2888

Bingen
Hotel-Restaurant Krone
Rheinkai 19
☎ 06721 17016

Boppard
Bellevue
Rheinallee 41
☎ 06742 2081
Elegant, highly regarded, family-run

Hotel Restaurant Rebstock
Rheinallee 41
☎ 06742 2671

Oberwesel
Hotel Gertum (garni)
Schaarplatz 18
☎ 06744 1520
Central near ship-station.

Burghotel Auf Schönburg
Schönburg
☎ 06744 7027

Rüdesheim
Gasthof Krancher
Eibinger-Oberstrasse 4
☎ 06722 2762
Short walk from centre, beside
vineyards; good food and own wine.

St Goar
Zur Traube
Heerstrasse 75
☎ 06741 7511

St Goarshausen
Pohl's Rheinhotel Adler
Bahnhofstrasse
☎ 06771 2613
Good middle-class hotel on front.

Tourist Information Offices

Bacharach
Oberstrasse 1
D-6533 Bacharach
☎ 06743 2968

Bad Kreuznach
Kurhaus
D-6550 Bad Kreuznach
☎ 0671 9 23 25

Bingen
Rheinkai 21
D-6530 Bingen
☎ 06721 1 42 69

Boppard
Karmeliterstrasse 2
D-5407 Boppard
☎ 06742 5081

Braubach
Rathausstrasse 8
D-5423 Braubach
☎ 12627 203

Oberwesel
Rathausstrasse 5
D-6532 Oberwesel
☎ 06744 1521

Rüdesheim
Rheinstrasse 16
D-6200 Rüdesheim
☎ 06722 2962

St Goar
Heerstrasse 120, Postfach 48
D-5401 St Goar am Rhein
☎ 06741 383

St Goarshausen
Bahnhofstrasse
D-5422 St Goarshausen
☎ 06771 427

5

THE RHEINGAU
AND RHEINHESSEN

The Rheingau: Rüdesheim to Mainz

Between Rüdesheim and the great city of Mainz the river Rhine shows a striking change of direction. The reason is again geological. At Mainz the river, which has been flowing broadly for many miles through the Rhine plain in a northerly course, suddenly comes up against the first outlying strata of the Taunus hills, part of the Rhenish Schist Uplands. So it runs along a westerly course until it finds the point — at Bingen — where it can break through the slate, however narrow and confined the channel.

This section is not so dramatic and spectacular as the Rhine gorge, yet throughout its history it has been specially valued and revered. The Rheingau, the land on the north bank, not only faces south as it gently slopes from the Taunus hills to the Rhine, but the Taunus shields it from the north winds, as well as having a fertile soil with the very characteristics on which the Riesling grape thrives. This is Germany's land of early spring and blossom-time.

In German the word *gau* has an old-fashioned flavour. Nowadays it means a region or district in a traditional sort of sense rather than a formal administrative unit. But its ancient meaning is of 'lands lying by the water' — ideal for settlement, so throughout history the Rheingau land has always been prized and coveted.

Many of its treasures and delights are not paraded on the riverfront, but shelter in the hinterland. So for the visitor who has travelled up the Rhine by ship, it is worth while to make an excursion from, say, Rüdesheim. Visitors using their own transport should make a Rheingau exploration that does not confine them only to the riverside road B42, but takes them on to sample the picturesque minor roads that penetrate north into famed and historic wine-growing districts.

EXCURSION BY ROAD FROM RÜDESHEIM

From central Rüdesheim take Grabenstrasse (just beyond the Adlerturm fortification-tower) that leads north into the access road signposted to the Niederwald Monument. Pass the *Krankenhaus* (hospital) on the right, continuing until a road branches off right marked Klosterweg leading up to St Hildegard's Abbey, set among vineyards only 2km (1$^1/_2$ miles) from the town. The terrace in front of the abbey church affords a fine view. This convent is an early twentieth-century building which houses an institution founded in 1165, and the nuns still observe the strict Benedictine rule.

From the convent, return downhill by Theodor Heuss-Strasse to cross under the railway, turn left and take the Wiesbaden road B42 east for 14km (9 miles) to **Eltville**, the oldest town of the Rheingau region, which obtained municipal rights in 1332. Eltville was the residence of the Electoral Archbishops of Mainz in the fourteenth and fifteenth centuries. Of the Electoral Castle only the *Wohnturm*, a square, four-storey residential tower of the fourteenth-century, is well-preserved. It now houses a Gutenberg Memorial as Eltville was one of the oldest printing centres and turned out some distinguished work in the fifteenth century. Gutenberg, the inventor of printing, incurred enmity and envy in his native Mainz, but was given residence here, a pension, and a court-title of honour by the Prince-Archbishop of Mainz. In the vicinity are impressive houses of the nobility and court officials. Of the extensive town fortifications the Martinstor, St Martin's Gate, and remains of battlemented walls survive. The old town's alleyways in the neighbourhood of the church repay a visit for their picturesque half-timbered dwellings and baroque buildings.

From Eltville take the exit north for **Kiedrich**, a good example of a distinguished wine-village in Gothic style. The furnishings of its handsome towering late-Gothic parish church of St Valentine, formerly a place of pilgrimage, are worth seeing. In particular, the 'Kiedricher Madonna' under the rood screen of 1340 ranks among the most outstanding achievements of German sculpture of the fourteenth-century. Here too music lovers can hear one of the oldest German church-organs and also hear choral singing of Latin liturgical hymns in the centuries-old Mainzer tradition of Gregorian chant. To crown the visit, Kiedrich, home of the Kiedricher Sandgrube wine, is an excellent place for a wine-tasting halt.

From Kiedrich take the road for 5km (3 miles) west to Kloster Eberbach in its sheltered valley. For centuries visitors have been attracted there by the beauty of its setting — and the excellence of its wines. In the high medieval period this was one of the Cistercians'

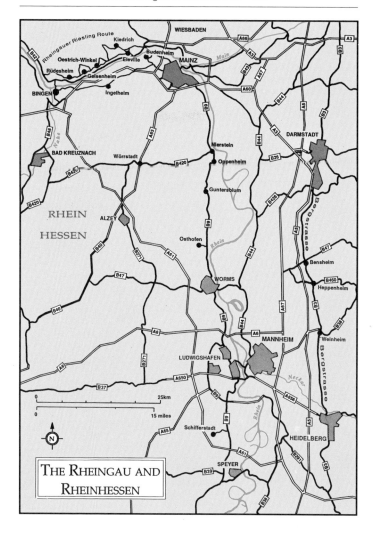

THE RHEINGAU AND
RHEINHESSEN

most important abbeys. It was founded in 1135 and its church consecrated in 1186. The order's concept of simplicity and discipline is reflected in the unadorned pure, and impressive, line of their Romanesque architecture. The whole abbey complex is surrounded by a wall 1km in length. Historically, its 300 monks and lay brothers ran a hospital, planted vines and over the years produced wine of such distinction that even a century later they had trade agencies for its distribution throughout the country and later throughout Europe. They even exported wine to England in their own ships. In common with others the monastery was secularised in 1803 and became a state domain of Hessen. It is now a state wine-estate. One of its sights today is the great wine-pressing house converted from the former hospital in the seventeenth century; it is a museum for the huge wine-presses and vats used in those days.

From Eberbach return to the main road B42 at Hattenheim, then to head west towards Winkel. **Hattenheim** itself is another picturesque little town, having one of the most attractive village squares in the region with slate-roofed, gable-ended houses that are dominated by the residential tower of its old castle. Here the Rhine is some 680m (2,231ft) from one shore to the other. After 4km ($2^1/_2$ miles) the road reaches **Oestrich**, with its numerous half-timbered houses of many types, and its lofty timber Rhine crane of 1744 on the riverfront. This was once the means of loading wine barrels from Kloster Eberbach into river vessels bound for Köln, but now stands as the town's emblem and landmark. A walk through Oestrich's little streets is like strolling through a different century; the half-timbered houses are adorned with so many quaint oriels, ornate gables, courtyard-entrances with coats-of-arms and inscribed scrolls. Not least, on the waterfront, one of Germany's most attractive inns and restaurants, the Schwan (Swan), with its Rhine-front terrace, beckons.

Nowadays neighbouring **Winkel** is linked to make up the twin town of Oestrich-Winkel. Winkel possesses what is claimed to be Germany's oldest stone-built dwelling house, the eleventh- or twelfth-century Graues Haus (Grey House) at Graue-gasse 8.

From Winkel two minor roads lead north to destinations of major interest. From the centre of Winkel a long avenue lined with poplar trees leads north into the wooded hills where lies the Rheingau's largest estate. Schloss Vollrads, the wine-domain of the Matuschka-Greiffenklau family, is famed both for its distinguished wines and for its picturesque baroque residence built of red sandstone and its fourteenth-century central tower or keep.

From the riverside road further west in Winkel runs another minor road heading first in a northerly direction then curving round to where another renowned wine-estate occupies a dramatic hill-top site that dominates the landscape. Schloss Johannisberg was formerly a monastery — the first such in the Rheingau, being an eleventh-century Benedictine foundation. As for the wine estate, legend relates that it was Charlemagne himself who from his palace at Ingelheim on the south side of the Rhine recognised the potential

Named Scenic Tourist Routes

Germany has many designated tourist routes, the best known being the **Romantic Road** from the Franconian Main river to the Alps. Several exist in the Rhine-Mosel region. The **Mosel Weinstrasse** (Mosel Wine Route) explains itself, is the name given to road B53 as it winds along the bends and loops of the river, sometimes on one side, sometimes on the other.

The main roads which run along both sides of the Rhine are most scenic. But the roads, railway lines and the riverside towns themselves are all strictly constrained within the narrow ribbon-like shelf of level ground that lies between the river and the steep slopes of the Rhine Gorge. So the Rhine-side roads, albeit undoubtedly scenic, are hardly routes to be enjoyed at a leisurely pace. The designated tourist routes take you away from the pressure of modern traffic alongside the river. Meandering like the old-time country roads, they are at times by the river, at times on the valley floor, at times climbing the lower slopes to reach a castle or a viewpoint, at times running up the valley of a tributary and even at times running on the level of the plateau itself. As they twist and turn they offer a remarkable series of sudden, breathtaking views of the river down below, the vine slopes, or the woodland slopes and the hamlets on the great rolling landscape of the plateau. The Rhine Gorge features two important tourist routes: the **Rheingoldstrasse** on the Rhine's west bank from Rhens to Rheindiebach near Trechtinghausen, and the **Loreley Burgenstrasse** from Bornhofen to Rüdesheim on the east bank. The **Rheingauer Riesling Route** which begins at Rüdesheim forms the basis of the itinerary around the Rheingau. Illustrated leaflets and maps on these routes can be obtained from tourist information offices in the area.

of the site and decreed it should be planted with vines. It did not receive the name by which it is now known world-wide, however, until the early twelfth century when the Benedictines from Mainz built the monastery here and its abbey church — a basilica which they consecrated to John the Baptist. That abbey church, a casualty in World War II, has since been reconstructed in its original Romanesque style as a pillared basilica.

The castle on the monastery site has had several owners. It was built in 1757-9 for the Prince Abbot of Fulda, and the estate is credited with the chance discovery of the magnificent properties of the quality wine known as *Trockenbeerenauslese*, made from grapes allowed to hang on the vine to shrink partly by the sun and partly by the attack of a beneficent mould, known to botanists as *Botrytis cinerea* and to German wine-growers as *Edelfäule* — 'the noble rot'. Permission to start the harvest had to be obtained from the Abbot at Fulda, but one year the messenger was seriously delayed and by the time he arrived the grapes had been attacked by mould. However, they completed the harvest and to their surprise the wine was found to be of marvellous quality. The castle's cellars have a magnificent collection of rare wine casks and bottles. Since 1810 the estate has belonged to the Metternich family, descendants of the Chancellor of Austria at that time. Last but not least, the view from the castle terrace is exceptional, even for this part of Germany.

The road south from Schloss Johannisberg rejoins road B42 near **Geisenheim**, another ancient town where tolls were once collected from traffic that used the land portage to bypass the rapids at Bingen. In the town are many manor houses of the nobility and churchmen of the sixteenth to eighteenth centuries. Of these Schloss Schönborn is admired as particularly picturesque, a Rhineland manor house in late Gothic style. It was the place where the details were hammered out for the Treaty of Westphalia which finally ended the Thirty Years' War that had torn Germany apart and ruined towns and countryside. In front of the town's townhall grows a lime tree of immense age — mentioned in the sixteenth century — beneath which justice was dispensed at one time. Because of it, Geisenheim's annual festival is known as the Lindenfest (Lime Tree Festival) held on the second Sunday of July. Nowadays Geisenheim is a name respected throughout the world, as the home during the past century of a great teaching and research institute for viticulture and horticulture, where many modern hybrid varieties of grapes for winemaking have been developed.

From Geisenheim it is only 2km ($1^1/_4$ miles) back to Rüdesheim.

Public Transport Options Excursions by bus can be made from Rüdesheim covering the general outline of the above route. (Further information from the local tourist office). The scheduled Rhine excursion ships call at Eltville. German Rail train services between Koblenz and Wiesbaden have regular stops (at approximately hourly intervals) at Rüdesheim, Geisenheim, Oestrich-Winkel, Hattenheim and Eltville. (DB Timetable No 611.)

Walking and Hiking: For visitors interested in walking or hiking there is a walking trail from Rüdesheim (or from Assmannshausen or even

Local wines may be bought directly from the vineyard

A traditional old wine press makes an attractive roadside feature

Lorch), signposted and kept in good order, known as the *Rheingauer Riesling-Pfad* (Rheingau Riesling Trail) which covers approximately the same route as the car-route on minor roads just described. It makes use of footpaths in the wine-estates etc. The trail is marked with signposts bearing the emblem of a gold Rhine-wine glass on a green background. A detailed description of the route, including a detailed map at 1.5cm per km (approx 1in=1 mile) can be obtained from the local or regional tourist offices. The map is sufficiently detailed and clear that even if an English version is not available it is still helpful to non-German speakers. The description divides the total route (from Lorch on the Rhine to Hochheim on the Main) into six day-walks varying from 12km ($7^1/_2$ miles) to 24km (15 miles).

The above road excursion dealt not only with places in the Rheingau hinterland but also with many of the wine villages on road B42 between Rüdesheim and Eltville. A few however were omitted which lie on sections of B42 which were by-passed.

Passengers on the excursion- or cruise-ship might have observed the operation of quite a useful ferry-service between the Rheingau and Rheinhessen shores of the river, some $7^1/_2$km ($4^3/_4$ miles) upstream from Rüdesheim. It plies between the old wine-village of Mittelheim, now incorporated into Oestrich-Winkel, on the north shore and Ingelheim-Nord on the south shore of the river. (Ingelheim is dealt with in the next section). Despite the busy riverside road nearby, **Mittelheim** with its poplar trees, meadows and country gardens preserves an air of seclusion; and even more so, among the vines, does its former abbey-church of St Agidienkirche, the Rheingau's oldest Romanesque church.

The previous excursion, by passing direct from Eberbach to Hattenheim, omitted any visit to **Erbach**, which lies just north of B42 between Hattenheim and Eltville (in which it is now incorporated). Coming from the west the visitor first meets Schloss Reinhardshausen, which is still owned by the Hohenzollern family. Before the castle however, by the roadside between the two villages can be seen a little fountain carved out of red sandstone that bears a name revered by lovers of Rhine wines, the Marcobrunnen (boundary fountain). It gave its name to a narrow strip of vineyard near the river which is one of the Rheingau's most distinguished sites, having produced the superlative Marcobrunner wines for centuries. Oddly enough, the owners who share it cannot agree on its spelling, which appears on some labels with 'c', on others with 'k'.

Further east (upstream) from Eltville lies the first of the suburbs of Wiesbaden, **Schierstein**, another old wine-village set in vineyards and orchards. It has a sizeable Rhine harbour just short of the main bridge carrying the A643 *Autobahn* across the Rhine to link Wiesbaden on the north bank with Mainz on the south. The bridge also marks the point at which the Rhine's change of direction again becomes perceptible in a gentle curve; Wiesbaden and Mainz mark the limit of the long east-west axis.

Just 2km (1^1/$_4$ mile) upstream from the bridge are the landing stages of **Biebrich**, Wiesbaden's Rhine-side up-market suburb and ancient ferry station. Its famous seventeenth/eighteenth-century castle — whose builders are said to have followed the plans of the renowned Viennese architect Fischer von Erlach — faces the Rhine. Immediately behind it runs extensive public parkland.

Wiesbaden owes its repute to the hot springs which were known and used by the Romans and which led to its existence as a spa. Of its twenty-six springs there is one, the Kochbrunnen, which on its own brings a half-million litres (100,000 gallons) of warm saline water to the surface every day. This together with its climatic advantages no doubt in turn influenced its choice as the second residence of the princes of Hessen-Nassau early in the eighteenth century. Finally in 1744 Wiesbaden became the capital of the Nassau realm. Today it is the seat of government for the state of Hessen.

The city itself has not the historic atmosphere of some of Germany's old cities, being largely a product of the nineteenth and twentieth centuries. Its attraction lies mainly in the magnificence of its *Kurhaus* (spa centre) with its complex of supporting buildings all in dignified neo-classical style. There is also the grandeur and majestic style of the surrounding parkland and gardens; the elegance of the neighbouring streets where hotels, cafés and stylish shops were once the preserve of prominent figures of their day. The streets still have style and considerable allure, Wilhelmstrasse being in particular famed as one of Europe' most elegant shopping streets — and for meeting in cafés. And the city caters well for all the arts in a rich annual programme of cultural and social events.

The oldest public building is the old town hall, of 1609, with an upper storey of two centuries later. The Stadtschloss, really a palace in classical style, now houses the state parliament. But the old Marktbrunnen, (market fountain) in front of it has stood there for 400 years. The city's most stylish residential area is to the north where the slopes and woods of the Taunus hills touch the city's verge. There too is the hill called the Neroberg where there is a splendid swimming-pool; on the same hill stands a chapel crowned with gilt onion-domes known as the Greek Chapel, or sometimes as the Russian, from the nationality of the young wife in whose memory it was erected by one of the Dukes of Nassau. Visitors to the Neroberg can be conveyed there by an antique hydraulically operated cogwheel railway.

South-east of Wiesbaden by some 10km (6 miles) and to the east of Mainz is a charming small wine-town that is classed among the great names of the Rheingau, although in fact it does not lie on the banks of the Rhine but on the north bank of the Rhine's large tributary, the Main. **Hochheim** is a most interesting phenomenon, in that far to the east of the Rheingau proper, the village is set in an island of vineyards in the midst of a farming and fruitgrowing landscape. Yet these vineyards produce wines with the characteristics typical of the Rheingau villages on the classic slopes further west. It was the wines of this village that captivated the taste of Queen Victoria when she visited this region in the mid-nineteenth century, which in turn led to German white wines becoming fashionable in English society — and for an abbreviated version of the village's name, 'Hock', becoming an English term for German white wine. It is not inappropriate that a vineyard sited between the town and the river is named after the queen 'Königin Victoriaberg'.

Rheinhessen: Bingen to Mainz & Worms

Many visitors find the names of the regions in this part of Germany somewhat confusing. The Rheingau that lies north of the river is part of the state of Hessen, while the region lying south of the river, known as Rheinhessen, does not lie in the state of Hessen but is part of the state of Rheinland-Pfalz (of which the Mosel, Eifel, Hunsrück and left-bank Mittelrhein are also parts).

Rheinhessen differs physically from the districts of the Mosel, Rhine gorge and Rheingau by being a landscape of gentle, fertile rolling country. Sheltered from bad weather by the Hunsrück in the west, the Taunus to the north and the Odenwald to the east, it has a mild, temperate climate. It is splendid agricultural country, and as the soil also suits vine-growing, vines flourish here bountifully. Rheinhessen and its neighbouring region to the south, Rheinpfalz, are the most productive wine regions in all Germany, and Rheinhessen leads the export market. But its fine-grained soil does not favour the Riesling grape; only 5 per cent of the vines here are Riesling, and these thrive best and derive their spicey tang on the red sandstone soil along the Rhine front. But the vast majority of its inland wines, made from Müller-Thurgau and Silvaner vines, are mild, gentle, palatable table-wines.

Rheinhessen has played quite a major part in German history for a region of its modest size (600 square miles). This is illustrated by

Traditional casks in a Rheinhessen wine cellar

The fortified church at Ober-Ingelheim

Ingelheim, 10km (6 miles) from Bingen and almost halfway between Bingen and Mainz (by *Autobahn* A60 or by train — DB Timetable 600).

This little town first gained importance in the reign of Charlemagne when in 788AD it was the scene of an Imperial Assembly. Later the great emperor built the Kaiser-Pfalz, his favourite Imperial Palace, here in Nieder-Ingelheim, and for many centuries the surrounding area was an imperial domain. It was heavily fortified some centuries later by the great Emperor Friedrich I, nicknamed 'Barbarossa', but scant remnants of its walls remain.

Charlemagne also introduced to the region the Blaue Spät-Burgunder grape (the classic *pinot noir* of Burgundy). The town is still known as the 'Red wine town' in a region where red-wine only amounts to 5 per cent of wine production. In the lower town is also the baroque Roman Catholic parish church. There are some remains of a carolingian bath, and of a Roman acquaduct.

Higher up in **Ober-Ingelheim** is the more interesting *Burgkirche,* or *Wehrkirche,* meaning in either case 'fortified church'. Ober-Ingelheim in the fourteenth and fifteenth centuries was where the imperial court of appeal sat. Not surprisingly, the little town was well fortified and substantial parts of the defences remain to give a fair idea of how it once was. The fourteenth- fifteenth-century *Burgkirche,* for instance, has a ring wall round its fortified churchyard and clearly formed part of the defences of the town.

Among the crops of this fertile region which may surprise the visitor is asparagus. In the asparagus 'season' all catering establishments make quite a feature of dishes involving the fresh local delicacy — and will recommend a local wine to accompany it.

Ingelheim is a convenient centre for excursions with a Rhine ferry from Ingelheim-Nord, $3^1/_2$km (2 miles) north of the town centre, to Mittelheim (part of Oestrich-Winkel) in the Rheingau.

Mainz is just 15km (9miles) from Ingelheim. Mainz's place in European history extends beyond two thousand years. Celtic tribes settled here five hundred years BC, then in 38BC the Romans established a legionary camp which they later extended to a fortress, accommodating two legions, as its strategic importance became evident. *Mogontiacum,* the name given by Romans, was the garrison-town of the famous Twenty-Second Legion for 300 years. Very interesting and extensive relics of this era are to be found in the Römisch-Germanisches Zentralmuseum, which has a research institute with a world reputation for restoring and interpreting objects recovered from excavation. Parts of the stonework that supported a Roman acquaduct over the meadow in the Zahl valley still survives. In the square beside the State Parliament building (for Mainz is the

capital of Rheinland-Pfalz) stands the Jupitersäule, a pillar erected   ✳
by Roman merchants to the Emperor Nero.

The importance of Mainz in succeeding eras was no less. St
Boniface, the Anglo-Saxon missionary to Germany, who became
Mainz's bishop in the eighth century, consolidated this area's con-
version to Christianity. In the following centuries the Mainz arch-
bishopric was superior to dioceses over an area from Prague and
Chur to Verdun. In the thirteenth century it was a seat of imperial
congresses and many emperors were crowned here. Its archbishop
became an Electoral Prince of the German Empire, and 'Golden
Mainz' became recognised as its foremost city. As such of course it
underwent tribulations as well as triumphs, suffered destruction by
Swedish armies during the Thirty Years' War and by the French in
the following century.

Today the city lives up to its rich heritage. Its great cathedral of St   ▲
Martin lies a little back from modern buildings, yet dominates both
them and the Rhine front. The open squares in its immediate neighbourhood emphasize its impressive might and dignity. It succeeds in
harmonizing many periods and styles. It was started in the year 975
with its eastern end in romanesque style; the western end was
completed in the mid-thirteenth century. The baroque top was not
added to the great tower until the second half of the eighteenth
century. When visiting the cathdral, do not miss the cathedral
museum's beautiful exhibits.

In the Domplatz, by way of contrast, stands a colourful and richly   ✳
decorated Renaissance fountain dating from 1526.

One of the best views of the eastern end of the cathedral is from the
courtyard of the nearby Gutenberg Museum, housed in a magnifi-   🏠
cent baroque building with a modern extension.Here the city honours its citizen Johannes Gutenberg who invented printing with
movable type. The museum has an authentic reproduction of his
workshop. It also possesses one of the rare survivers of the hundred
or so copies he printed of his famous Bible. This extraordinary man
chose as his first project with his new invention a complete printing
of the Bible — which experts today still revere as one of the most
beautiful products of the printer's craft. The museum also exhibits
the development of printing from Gutenberg's day to this.

Just downstream from the building called the Deutschhaus where
the State Parliament meets is the splendid Kurfürstliches Schloss   🏛
(Palace of the Prince Electors), which was built in the seventeenth
and eighteenth centuries. Some of its formal apartments have been
restored in original style, while part of the building houses the
world-famous Roman-German Museum (already referred to) along   🏠

with its research departments.

But Mainz was never entirely devoted to formality and ceremony. It has always been and still is also a wine city. Here are the homes of many institutions concerned with the wine trade and the production of wine; and the headquarters of hundreds of wine distributors and also many producers of *Sekt* (or *Schaumwein*), the general German name for sparkling wines made by a champagne process. In the narrow alleys of the old town, with its fascinating restored half-timbered buildings, there is an abundance of *Kneipen*, *Weinstuben* and cafés — all dispensing wine, good cheer and the good-

The cathedral church of St Martin, Mainz

humoured joviality which is a characteristic of the Mainzer. The highlight of the year in Mainz is the celebration of Fastnacht, the carnival festival so beloved by all Rhinelanders, but of which they say the city is 'the Capital'.

EXCURSION TO THE WONNEGAU

The fertile triangle of territory that lies between Bingen, Mainz and Worms is generally known as the Wonnegau, or 'land of bliss'. It differs from most parts of Germany in its lack of woodlands, the intensity of its cultivation of vines, its fruit orchards (including peaches and apricots as well as the more usual cherries and pears) and the asparagus crops. Right at the heart of it is the little town of **Alzey**, 34km (21 miles) from Mainz. An excursion there on the road B40 gives a fair sample of the landscape — and also touches the little town of **Wörrstadt** with its old fortifications, its great elms and its Romanesque-Gothic St Laurence church.

Alzey is characterised by its charming late-renaissance town hall with its spiral-staircase turret and its frame of well preserved half-timbered other buildings at the Fischmarkt and the Rossmarkt (horse market) as well as in the Schlossgasse. The town was nearly totally destroyed by the French in the late seventeenth century, yet it still preserves much of the medieval town-walls, including a square tower and a town gate. Alzey had a moated keep of the Romanesque period, which was extended into a castle in later medieval times; this was restored at the beginning of the twentieth century with a rather romantic emphasis, yet it has a pleasing compact outline.

Public Transport Option: This excursion can very conveniently be carried out by train. Germany Rail runs a service from Mainz to Alzey at approximately hourly intervals, the trip taking about an hour, calling at Wörrstadt among other villages. (DB Timetable 655.)

MAINZ TO WORMS

Almost directly across the Rhine from Mainz is the mouth of another of its great tributaries, the river Main.

Keeping on the Rheinhessen side of the river, the old wine-village of **Nackenheim** lies about 12km ($7^1/_2$ miles) upstream from Mainz, just off road B9. Nackenheim was known as a wine-village in the seventh century, but to modern western Europeans it is perhaps now best-known as the home town of the twentieth-century dramatist Karl Zuckmayer. It has an attractive eighteenth-century town hall. Because of two tree-clad islands in the Rhine nearby it has in modern times become a favourite destination for those interested in water sports. In other respects it is in the shadow of its bigger neighbour Nierstein 5km (3 miles) further south.

Wholly framed in vineyards **Nierstein** is the largest wine-growing community on the Rhine with more than 1,000 hectares (2,470 acres) of vineyard, including some fine ones lying along a ridge of reddish slate-stone soil. However these are swamped by the great number of secondary vineyards contributing to the familiar *Grosslage* 'Gutes Domtal'. It has one or two handsome baroque residences of the local nobility in the market square, notably the stately Haxthauserhof. The Protestant church has a most impressive medieval fortified church-yard with a romanesque east gate to the market-place and at the south-west corner a Gothic round tower complete with battlements. The town's landmark is a watch-tower on a nearby hill. 3km (2 miles) away among the the the vineyards rises the lofty ruinous dungeon-keep of a former imperial castle, the Schwabsburg, which was sacked by the Spaniards in 1620 and finally destroyed in 1799. The town's old town hall houses two museums, one being a palaeontological collec-tion — from local excavations — of petrified animals, insects, plants; the other illustrates the development of Rhine shipping in the eighteenth- and nineteenth centuries.

Only $1^1/_2$km (1 mile) further on lies **Oppenheim** on the slopes above the Rhine bank, another name familiar from bottles of German table wines. This picturesque town is reputed to enjoy the sunniest locality on the Rhine and certainly its situation is lush not only with vineyards but in its riverside water meadows lined with poplars. The town itself is rich in half-timbered buildings and stylish old houses. Its St Katherinenkirche, started in 1262 and reputed to be the most important Gothic building on the Rhine between Strassbourg Minster and Köln Cathedral, is enhanced by the warmth of its red sandstone, and its superlative Gothic rose window. Behind is the Gothic chapel of St Michael with its ossuary or charnel house. Many of its skulls and bones date to the Thirty Years' War period. Above the church and town stand the ruins of Landskron castle, destroyed in 1118 but rebuilt as an imperial castle when the town became a free imperial city. It was laid waste in 1689, but the walls of the residential palace partially survive.

The town's life has centred around viticulture and the wine trade. For a century now its State Institute for Instruction and Research in Viticulture and Horticulture has contributed greatly to vine growing in Rheinhessen. Its museum illustrates the development of viticul-ture and all the technical processes including cellar-operations.

At Nierstein the river, the town and the main road were adjacent to one another, but by Oppenheim there is a decided gap between the river and road because of a long gradual curve in the course of the river and this gap increases as road B9 runs south in a fairly straight line through fertile wine growing country. **Guntersblum**, 8km (5 miles) south of Oppenheim, has many features reminiscent of earlier days and ways. A unique feature is the little town's *Kellerweg* (cellar road) a 1km stretch of continuous wine cellars built into the hillside, some of more than one storey, instead of being excavated underground as wine cellars normally are. This practice goes back more than three centuries to times when the watertable was too high for underground cellarage. A re-alignment of the Rhine took place in the early nineteenth century which helped the low-lying lands on both Rhine banks. It also gave rise — on the opposite, east bank — to the very large Rhine island of Kühkopf which is now an interesting wildlife conservation area and bird haunt that can be visited by ferry boat from the Guntersblum ferry pier.

The next place of interest is a short distance away from the Rhine and consequently missed by those who do this itinerary by river vessel. **Osthofen** lies little more than 1km ($^2/_3$ mile) west of the B9. Its landmark is the *Bergkirche* on the Goldberg vineyard hill, erected in 1747 on the ruins of an imperial twelfth-century castle-keep. Local tradition has it that subterranean passages once ran from it to Oppenheim's St Catherine's Church and to the cathedral in Worms! The Goldberg hill gives a fine view south in the direction of Worms.

Worms lies 7km ($4^1/_2$ miles) from the Osthofen crossroads. Halfway down that stretch the road is once more running alongside the Rhine. And just as Worms is reached, the Rhine is crossed by the Nibelungenbrücke which connects Worms and the Rheinhessen hinterland with the Odenwald region on the east side of the Rhine.

Worms is one of Germany's oldest cities. However, arriving there from the medieval wine towns in the Rheingau and the Wonnegau brings rather a cultural shock. For the Nibelungenbrücke is of pre-stressed concrete (the first such built over the Rhine) and is in keeping with the city's modern role as an important industrial city in chemicals and engineering, while still remaining a very important centre of the wine trade.

Worms existed as a Celtic settlement, was later the site of a Roman fort, and became the centre of a Christian bishopric in the fourth century. When the flood of Germanic tribe migrations swept the Romans away, Worms survived as the capital of the Burgundian kingdom in 413, but was destroyed by Attila's Huns less than a quarter-century later. As the name of the concrete Rhine-bridge reminds us, Burgundian Worms features largely in the ancient

German epic of the Nibelungs which Richard Wagner's music in modern times brought to the attention of a far wider world. On the Rhine front beside the landing stage stands a statue of Hagen throwing the Nibelungs' treasure hoard into the river.

In the European history books the city's name is associated with two great historical watersheds: the reign of Charlemagne and the era of Martin Luther's appearance to defend his teachings at the Reichstag's Diet (or congress) of 1521. The latter was only one of the more than a hundred such meetings that took place in this free imperial city during the Middle Ages. Not surprisingly, then, the attraction in Worms lies at the old town's centre: the cathedral church of Saints Peter and Paul, a monumental achievement of eleventh-twelfth-century high Romanesque architecture. The main portal of the church is of Gothic date and style, while the east choir's splendid high altar is baroque.

Just south-west of the cathedral beyond Andreas-strasse is St Magnus, the oldest Protestant church in south-west Germany, a tenth- to fourteenth-century Romanesque building. Immediately beyond it is the former twelfth- thirteenth-century Andreaskirche, which along with neighbouring buildings is now the Andreasstift municipal museum with displays of the archaeology and early history of Worms. There are special exhibits on Luther and on the Romans in Worms. The Andreas Ring, heading west, leads to the Judenfriedhof, Europe's largest and oldest Jewish cemetery, with memorial stones of eleventh- and twelfth-century date.

A little to the north of the cathedral square, in the Stephansgasse, is the Heylshof Art Foundation with its valuable collection of European art from the fifteenth- to nineteenth centuries. The collection was originally a private collection of the Baron von Heyl and is housed in a former Heyl family villa built and decorated in the Biedermeier style of mid-nineteenth century Germany.

From here walking west on Stephansgasse, you reach the garden-park in which stands the Luther Memorial, the world's greatest monument to the Reformation, erected in 1868 in the city where Martin Luther's defence of his theological theses took place in 1521 — generally regarded as a turning point in the history of Europe.

Continue north from here in the gardens to where Wilhelm-Leuschner-strasse comes in from the main railway station (from the left). Turn right into it and then left into Martinsgasse which proceeds north. Follow Martinsgasse to its intersection with Ludwigsplatz and Korngasse (running west-east, in which, further east, is the main post office). On the corner of Korngasse and the continuation north of Martinsgasse is another fine Romanesque church of eleventh- thirteenth-century date, the Martinskirche. From the church continue north on Martinsgasse, a one-way street, as it slowly curves round to Judengasse on the right. Medieval Worms had a large Jewish community which is thought to have been established there even in Roman times, and the eleventh-century synagogue in the Judengasse was probably the most important in all Europe. It was totally destoyed by arson in the Nazis' infamous 'Krystall-nacht' of terrorism in 1938, but it was fully rebuilt in 1961. Since 1970 the old Jewish quarter, old dwelling-houses as well as community buildings such as the Raschi Schule with its Judaica-Museum, has been systematically rehabilitated.

North from Judengasse, beyond the Berliner-ring, the road north leads to the vineyard landscape and the charming fourteenth- fifteenth-century Liebfrauenkirche. These forty acres of vineyard are often said to be the origin of the lakes of Liebfrauenmilch (or Liebfraumilch) wine which are exported all over the world. In fact the German Wine Law of 1971 permits any 'mild' tasting white wine from Rheinhessen, Nahe, Palatinate or Rheingau, made from Riesling, Silvaner or Müller-Thurgau grapes, to be called Liebfraumilch — provided it has passed the quality tests of course!

Public Transport Option: The excursion from Mainz to Worms can be readily undertaken by train on the service Mainz-Worms-Mannheim, with stops at Nackenheim, Nierstein, Oppenheim, Guntersblum and Osthofen; the journey Mainz-Worms takes about 45 minutes. (DB Timetable 660.)

Additional Information

Places of Interest

Alzey
Museum Alzey
Antoniterstr 41
Open: Tues-Sun 10am-12noon, 2-5pm

Geisenheim
Schloss Johannisberg
Visits to historic wine estate and castle by arrangement. Contact Geisenheim Tourist Office
☎ 06722 8021

Kiedrich
Kloster Eberbach
4km from Kiedrich
Open for visits to historic cellars of State Hessen

Mainz
Gutenberg Museum
Liebfrauenplatz 5
Open: Tues-Sat 10am-6pm, Sun 10am-1pm

Dom- u Diozesanmuseum
Domstrasse
Open: Mon, Tues, Wed, Fri 9am-12,
2-5pm, Thur, Sun 9am-12noon.

*Römisch-Germanisches
Zentralmuseum*
Kurfürstliches Schloss
Open: Tues-Sun 10am-6pm.
(Entrance free in all of these.)

Nierstein
Paläontologisches Museum
Altes Rathaus
Open: Sun 10am-1pm. (Groups by
appointment. ☎ 06133 58312).

Schiffer-museum
Altes Rathaus. Open summer by
appointment 9am-12noon
Tel 06133 5447.

Oppenheim
Deutsches Weinbaumuseum
Wormserstrasse 49
Open: daily except Mon, 1-5pm.
Guided tours by advance notice
☎ 06133/2544.

Wiesbaden
Städtisches Museum
Friedrich-Ebert-Allee
For opening hours enqure:
Info, Museum
☎ 06121 368 2187

Worms
Museum der Stadt (Andreasstift)
Weckerlingplatz
Open: daily (except Mon) 9am-
12noon, 2-5pm

Kunsthaus Heylshof (Art Foundation)
Stephansgasse 9
Open: May to Sept daily (except
Mon) 10am-5pm; Oct to April
Tues-Sat 2-4pm, Sun 10am-12noon,
2-4pm

Judaica Museum
Raschi-Haus
Open: daily (except Mon) 10am-
12noon, 2-5pm.

Hotels and Restaurants

Mainz
Novotel Mainz-Sud
Essenheimerstr 200
☎ 06131 361054
Conveniently reached from *Autobahn*

Wiesbaden
Hotel am Landeshaus
Moritz Str 51
☎ 06121 373041
Buffet breakfast

Restaurant Alt-Prag
41 Taunus Str
☎ 0621 52 04 02
Features Czech specialities

Worms
Central Hotel
Kammererstr 5
☎ 06241 54 58

Tourist InformationCentres

Mainz
Bahnhofstrasse 15, Postfach 4140
D-6500 Mainz 1
☎ 06131 23 37 41

Mannheim
Bahnhofplatz 1
D-6800 Mannheim 1
☎ 0621 101011

Wiesbaden
Rheinstrasse 15
Ecke Wilhelmstrasse
D-6200 Wiesbaden
☎ 06121 312847

Worms
Neumarkt 14
D-6520 Worms. ☎ 06241 25045

6

SPEYER AND HEIDELBERG

Two special excursion destinations lie south of the area covered by a classic Rhineland tour and the cities of Speyer and Heidelberg are deservedly popular with visitors.

Speyer

Speyer is commonly mentioned in the same breath as Mainz and Worms, for these three cities played an important role in the shaping of medieval Germany. This is underlined by their great early medieval cathedrals. Speyer is a regular calling place of the Rhine cruise vessels which travel from Amsterdam, Nijmegen or Köln to the Swiss port of Basel. Motorists also will find it is conveniently reached by *Autobahn* using A63 and A61 from Mainz (105km, 65 miles) or Worms (57km, 35 miles.)

Public Transport Option: By train Mainz is the key to the excursion, being readily accessible from all resorts in the Rhine gorge area. Take the same main line (DB Timetable 660) to Worms, but continue to Ludwigshafen. Change there for Speyer by way of Schifferstadt junction (Timetable 675).

Like Worms, Speyer has evidence of established settlement not only before Roman times but even before the German tribes of Vangiones and Nemetes under the leadership of Ariovistus crossed the Rhine in hordes and dispossessed the Celts. All early Roman references to the region of Speyer were of a substantial community of the Nemetes, *Civitas Nemetum.* It is only in the early sixth century that the name 'Spira' began to appear. A century later there is clear evidence that Speyer was the seat of a bishop, who in following centuries became the temporal ruler of the region. The influence of the bishopric and town multiplied when Konrad II, member of a family in the region of Speyer, became German king in 1024. By 1030 the foundation stone had been laid for the building of a cathedral in Speyer, but in 1294 the bishop surrendered most of his temporal powers in the city and it became one of the seven Free Imperial Cities of the Holy Roman Empire of the Germans.

The most obvious evidence today of Speyer's former political and economic importance is the surviving section of the old town's medieval city wall, the handsome thirteenth-century gate tower, the Altpörtel, which stands at the other end of Maximilian-strasse from the cathedral, near the point where Bahnhofstrasse cuts into Maximilianstrasse. It is one of the highest and most important city gates in Germany and was one of the sixty-eight towers of the city wall. The city's importance is also borne out by Speyer's record of having housed no less than fifty Imperial Diets in the medieval period. Two of these, the Diets of 1526 and 1529, were of European significance as they prepared the way for the splitting of the Christian Church. The Protestation of 1529 was the start of the split of reformers, who were to become known as Protestants, from the Roman Catholic Church.

In the War of the Palatinate Succession, Louis XIV of France's troops destroyed and burned down Speyer in 1689. The Altpörtel and the east end of the cathedral were all that survived of the city's core. Ten years later when the rebuilding was started the original outline of the city centre was retained — and the city's axis maintained between the cathedral and the Altpörtel. Newer public buildings of that period were in baroque style, such as the town hall of 1720, the Dreifaltigkeitskirche (Trinity Church) of 1701-17 and the Alte Münze (Old Mint) of 1748.

The French Revolutionary invasions of 1797 made Speyer — and all west-bank Rhineland — French. But in the post-Napoleonic War peace settlements the Pfalz am Rhein (Palatinate) was attached to the kingdom of Bavaria, and Speyer became the Palatinate capital. So in the nineteenth century it was predominantly an administrative centre. It was not until the present century that it began to play a more prominent role in economy and industry under the influence of the neighbouring industrial city and Rhine port of Ludwigshafen. Today this continues and, as a cultural centre in south-west Germany, Speyer is also a residential area for commuters who work in nearby Mannheim/Ludwigshafen.

A city walk almost inevitably starts at one end or the other of Maximilianstrasse, depending on whether you arrive from the railway station or from the Rhine promenade and ship station. Assuming the latter, the first monument is the mighty six-towered Roman-

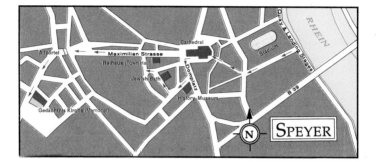

esque cathedral which was founded in 1030 by the first king and emperor, Konrad II. An approach through the cathedral gardens at its east end introduces sculptures of the dynasty of emperors who were responsible for its construction.

In the west porch are statues of the eight kings of Germany and emperors of the Holy Roman Empire who were buried in the imperial vault; some of the tombs were pillaged by French invaders in 1689. The great lofty church, with what seem immensely tall and slender pillars supporting the cross-vaulted ceiling, is the greatest of all Europe's Romanesque ecclesiastical buildings. The crypt is the largest in Germany, spacious and fine with groined vaulting and the contrasting dark red and white stonework of its arches. But most attractive of all is the lovely east end of the cathedral, the part which survived 1689 unscathed, with its raised Königschor (Royal Choir), twin towers, and original romanesque transept.

Immediately in front of the cathedral stands what resembles an outsize baptismal font, the sixteenth-century *Domnapf*, a sandstone basin which traditionally was filled with wine for the citizens on the occasion of a new bishop's ordination, but is said originally to have been the boundary stone between the jurisdiction of the city from that of the bishop. Turning left (south) down the Domplatz you find the Historisches Museum der Pfalz (Historic Museum of the Palatinate) with its fascinating collections from prehistoric and Roman sites. There are medieval art treasures — and above all the dramatic conical 'Golden Hat', which is a masterpiece of the goldsmith's craft and believed to be associated with fertility cults.

A short distance away, by way of Gross-Pfassengasse and Judengasse is the Synagogen-Judenhof site, the area of the Jewish quarter in the eleventh century where the Jewish Bath is to be found. This is the ritual cleansing bath that was constructed here before 1128 as part of the synagogue of that era. Today it lies nearly 10m (33ft) below the level of the small garden which surrounds it and is now a memorial. Retracing your steps to Webergasse, this leads (on the right) into the principal thoroughfare, Maximilianstrasse, just beside the town hall. This is a typical late baroque building (1712-26) that replaced its fifteenth-century predecessor destroyed in 1689. Inside it is worthwhile visiting the *Ratssaal* (Council Chamber) which is decorated and furnished in early rococo style.

From the town hall a walk down the length of the broad Maximilianstrasse illustrates how this has been the city's axis for nearly a thousand years, with houses of various ages on both sides of the street. At the west end is the Altpörtel, one of Germany's tallest (55m, 180ft high) and most important city gates, which is referred to as early as 1176. It was formerly the city's main western gateway. The topmost storey with its late-Gothic tracery parapet and arcaded gallery was added in 1512-14; the steep roof and crowning lantern are of 1708. Fortunately the tower escaped the razing of the city in 1689 and remains as a surviver of the medieval town defences. From the gallery of the tower there is a splendid bird's-eye view of the town. After interior reconstruction a permanent display illustrates the history of the Altpörtel and the city's fortifications.

On leaving the Altpörtel it is only a short walk down Gilgenstrasse, half-left, to the Gedächtniskirche (Memorial Church), erected at the turn of the twentieth century as a memorial to the historic Protestation at the 1529 Imperial Diet in Speyer. This neo-Gothic church with the highest tower (100m, 328ft) in Speyer is regarded as a distinguished artistic achievement of modern times worthy to rank with its predecessors.

Heidelberg

Heidelberg does not lie on the Rhine, but on another of its tributaries, the Neckar. Yet such is its charisma and romantic appeal that most visitors to the Rhineland decide to include the city. Passengers on the K-D Rhine cruise-ships from Holland (or Köln) to Basel in Switzerland can pause at Mannheim on the Rhine to make an excursion to Heidelberg, just 18km (11 miles) away. The city — on a commanding natural site — has throughout the centuries had a great impact on history, music, literature, drama and education.

The city lies where the river Neckar has just broken through the Odenwald hill country on the north-east and east into a fairly spacious basin that leads into the upper Rhine plain. The last outriders of the Odenwald make a magnificent back drop to the city's setting in the form of two shapely hills one on each side of the Neckar.

These are the 440m (1,444ft) high Heiligenberg (Saints' Hill) to the north and the 568m (1,864ft) Königstuhl (Royal Throne) to the south, both providing citizens and visitors with areas for recreation. This situation shields Heidelberg from chill northerly winds. In any case it lies at the southern end of a remarkable climatic phenomenon associated with the *Bergstrasse* or Mountain Road. This ancient road starts about Darmstadt, south of both Wiesbaden and Frankfurt, and runs along the edge of the Odenwald's hilly forest slopes to Heidelberg. Year after year it is along this road that spring first arrives in Germany. People come from other regions at end of March to see the blossoming of peach, almond and apricot in the orchards, followed in succession by cherry and plum, finally apple and pear.

Those who have visited the Rhine Gorge and then the Rheingau by private transport, should take the A671 from Wiesbaden or A60 from Mainz until these merge at the *Autobahn Dreieck* (literally, 'triangle' but on an *Autobahn* a three-road junction) named Mainspitz. From there continue on the A60 to the Rüsselsheimer Dreieck, then the A67 for Darmstadt. There, if pushed for time, you may continue south on *Autobahn* A5; but it is far more interesting to take road B3 from south of Eberstadt. This is the *Bergstrasse* which runs via Bensheim, Heppenheim and Weinheim to Heidelberg (61km, 38 miles, from Darmstadt, 106km, 66 miles, from Wiesbaden). Motorists coming from Speyer (30km, 18 miles) will find it more interesting to take road B39 east across the Rhine and remain on it until its junction with the southern part of the *Bergstrasse*. There turn left (north) to Heidelberg.

Thanks to Heidelberg's geographical position it is favoured with good transport routes. But it is also important for motorists to realise there is a complex network of *Autobahn* routes to the west serving the big industrial conurbations of Mannheim-Ludwigshafen on the Rhine plain. It is important that motorists in this region are clear in advance as to which *Autobahn* or federal road they mean to use and to be sure of following the correct road numbers.

Public Transport Option: Heidelberg is well-served by rail from the Rhineland further north. Southward from Mainz there is the option of travelling on the mainline west-bank line via Worms and Mannheim (DB Timetable 660 and 702) or via Darmstadt (DB Timetable 552) and thence by way of the *Bergstrasse* country (ie by Bensheim, Heppenheim and Weinheim) using DB Timetable 550. As the route on Timetable 550 actually starts from Frankfurt Hauptbahnhof this is an obvious choice for visitors to Heidelberg who have arrived by air at Frankfurt Airport. A special limousine transfer service direct from the airport (check-in at the meeting point in airport Hall B) to

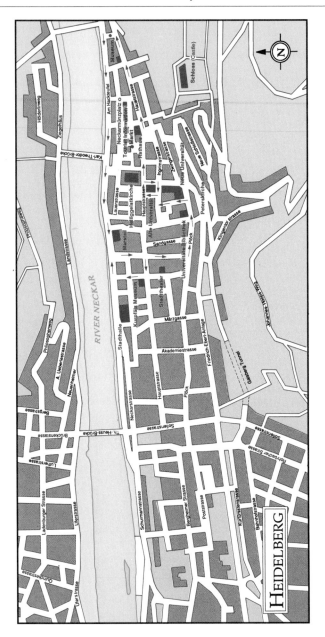

The elaborate gable of the Ritter, now a hotel, Heidelberg

Heidelberg's busy pedestrianised high street

your hotel in Heidelberg can be arranged as part of the hotel booking. The journey only takes an hour.

A CITY WALK IN HEIDELBERG

For a considerable number of years the old town has been a pedestrian precinct, with parking in the city fringes, north and south. Even judged by the generous standards throughout Germany, the free information leaflets and maps from the Heidelberg tourist information office are particularly helpful and detailed, so a call there, or a previous contact by letter, should be a priority.

The traditional start for a city-walk (of about two hour's duration) is in front of the Old University, at the Löwenbrunnen (Lion's Fountain) in University Square off the Hauptstrasse, the principal street of the city. For visitors arriving by train, bus No 10 or 11 from the main station will take them to Universitätsplatz.

The lion of the fountain was a heraldic emblem of the Palatinate. Although in the nineteenth century Heidelberg was incorporated into the Grand Duchy of Baden and in the twentieth has become part of the state of Baden-Württemberg, it was in previous centuries part of the Pfalz, or Palatinate, on the west bank of the Rhine, which is now in the modern state of Rheinland-Pfalz.

Heidelberg is the oldest of the German universities, having been founded in 1386 by the Count Palatine, Ruprecht I, one of the seven imperial Prince Electors of that time. It played a considerable role in the rise of humanist studies and in the Reformation movement, and later it was influential in the struggle between Lutherans and Calvinists. The Old University building was erected 1712-28 (Heidelberg having been virtually destroyed in 1689-93 after its capture by the French). There is a New University building in the immediate neighbourhood of the old, erected in 1930-2 with contributions to its building fund coming from many American sources.

In Augustinergasse, which lies to the east of the Old University building and runs at right angles to the Hauptstrasse, is the Studentenkarzer — the historic jail where troublesome students were locked up during the century and a half before World War I. Its rooms are famed for the graffiti which temporary residents contributed to the decor. A few steps further south is the Hexenturm (Witches' Tower) which is almost the sole surviving part of the old city wall. Leaving by the gate to the south you then face the Collegium Academicum of 1750 which has had a chequered career as a Jesuit seminary, school, clinic, barracks and is now a student residence. Head east along Seminarstrasse and turn left into Schulgasse to find the Jesuit Church and Seminary of 1712-50, to which the tower was added in the nineteenth century.

From the church head north by Kettengasse back into Haupt-strasse and turn right. Here there are some interesting buildings to admire — and many tempting shop windows to be scanned as well! At the Kettengasse corner is a handsomely decorated burgher's dwelling of the eighteenth century. Next on the right is the splendid renaissance mansion Haus zum Ritter, now a hotel, the only mansion to survive the destruction of 1689; it was built in 1592 by a cloth-merchant, who was a French Huguenot refugee. Its Renaissance façade has the figure of the knight St George. Opposite the Ritter is the Heiliggeistkirche (Church of the Holy Spirit) built in 1399-1441, which was the burial place of the Electors, although the only surviv-ing tomb is of King Ruprecht and his wife. This was the church in which the priceless Palatinate library was kept until 1628, when Count Tilly, commander of the conquering army of the Catholic League in the Thirty Year's War, carried it off as a present to the Vatican. In 1816 Pope Pius VII returned many of the precious German manuscripts to Heidelberg.

Next to the church is the Marktplatz with its fountain of Hercules, where in the fifteenth century both witches and heretics were burned. Immediately beyond the square, still on the left side of Hauptstrasse, is the town hall (1701). Across the Hauptstrasse, at the corner of the Kornmarkt, is the 'Prince Carl', now a town hall annexe but formerly (1788-1915) an inn whose guests included Mark Twain, Bismarck and Kaiser Wilhelm I when he was prince. The Kornmarkt is a good place to be any evening just before 7pm, for at that time you can hear the town hall *glockenspiel* playing a selection of folk tunes. Cross the Kornmarkt from which there is a very good view up to the castle; from this square a funicular railway runs to the castle. Turning left from Kornmarkt you enter Karlstrasse where further east is the baroque Grossherzöglicher Palais (Grand Ducal Palace) in Karls-platz. Its reception rooms with period furniture have one of the finest interiors in the region, but as it is now an Academy of Sciences it is not open to the general public.

Crossing Karlsplatz back to Hauptstrasse you face the Palais Boisserée of 1742. Just beyond this to the east stand two notable buildings at No 213 and No 217, the taverns Zum Sepp'l and Zum Roten Ochsen (Red Ox Tavern), both historic student (and, in season, tourist!) drinking houses where you can find substantial quantities of beer, wholesome food and lots of atmosphere. Further along on the left is the Palais Weimar built in the eighteenth century by the city's commander but now housing ethnological collections, mainly of African origin. Finally Hauptstrasse ends with the Karlstor, a neo-classical city gate built in 1775 to honour the Elector Karl Theodor.

From the river front — no great distance from the Karlstor — there is a view of the barrier and locks which control the river level. Turning back west along the riverside walk you reach Neckarmünzplatz with a parking area for tour buses and the tourist information office (open during the season, 9am to 6.30pm). From the information office turn away from the immediate river front and walk along Obere Neckarstrasse so as to be on the right level to step onto the Brückentor, with its portcullis and twin towers capped with bell-shaped domes which are so emblematic of the city. The Alte Brücke is also known as the Karl-Theodor-Brücke after the Elector who had it built in 1786-8 as the first stone bridge over the Neckar. His statue stands on it, as well as one of Athena. At the far end of the bridge is another statue, that of its patron saint Johannes Nepomuk. From that end is one of the classic views of the city and castle.

Continue west along the riverfront until Grosse Mantelgasse cuts in from the left. At its corner is the building known as the Heuscheuer (barn) which was used to store taxes that were paid in kind; in recent time its interior has been remodelled into lecture halls. To its immediate west stands a much larger building, the Marstall, the former arsenal which is the modern students' refectory. Beyond that, in turn, is the picturesque Schiffgasse which leads back to the Hauptstrasse. In Schiffgasse is one of the most handsome of the baroque residences, dated 1752. Further west is a former eighteenth-century baroque mansion, the Palais Morass, with a handsome staircase so characteristic of that period. Originally built in 1712, it is now the Kurpfälzisches Museum (Palatinate Museum) with some wonderful exhibits. There are archaeological objects from the Roman era and earlier found locally, while on the artistic side the most precious object is probably the exquisite wooden altar on which is carved with such genial mastery Christ with his Twelve Apostles.

From the museum retrace your steps east on the Hauptstrasse, just short of where Schiffgasse comes in on the left, and turn right into Theaterstrasse. This leads through to the street called Plöck. Turn left and follow it to its end where, on the left, is the University Library, built at the beginning of this century; among other manuscripts it holds the Manesse Codex, a unique collection of medieval lyric poetry. Facing the library across the Plöck is the delightful late-Gothic Peterskirche (1485), with a romanesque tower which is thought to be part of an earlier church of twelfth-century date. This, the oldest parish church of the city, also serves the academic community. Its churchyard has tombstones of distinguished academic and civic figures of the fifteenth to nineteenth centuries.

Schloss Heidelberg dominates the Old Bridge over the river Neckar

From St Peter's it is a short walk along Grabengasse, opposite, to the Universitätsplatz from which the city walk began. But also from St Peter's by following the overhead arrows the ascent can be made by the serpentine Neue Schlossstrasse to the Heidelberg Schloss, which lies some 80m (262ft) higher up on the hillside of the Königstuhl. The easiest method of ascent is by walking along Hauptstrasse (or parallel alleys) east to the Kornmarkt to the lower station of the funicular railway which ascends to the castle, and indeed continues further to the summit of the Königstuhl. The more energetic can take a much more direct path also from near the Kornmarkt, known as the Burgweg. From this, when you stop to regain your breath, you can look down on splendid views of Heidelberg.

SCHLOSS HEIDELBERG

The castle is regarded as the most beautiful and impressive ruined castle in Germany. It certainly has a most romantic setting to which its warm sandstone and the gracious outline of its buildings make a telling contribution. The building was commenced by the same Ruprecht I who started the university. Extensive developments were made by his successors from the mid-sixteenth to early seventeenth century, and it was the residence of the Electors for some five centuries. Both town and castle were devastated in 1689-93 by the war fought by the armies of Louis XIV over the succession to the throne of the Palatinate. In 1720 the Elector Carl Philipp transferred his main residence to Mannheim and made it his capital.

The fortifications, the residential areas, domestic premises and palatial state apartments reflect the long period of occupation. One of the most lavish wings was rebuilt in 1889-1901. Nowadays all kinds of special events are organised at the castle: open-air theatre and concerts in the inner courtyard as part of the regular festivals, ballet in Schlossgarten or Königsaal (Royal Hall), the latter also being used for banquets. Needless to say it provides a splendid site for illuminations and fireworks on festive occasions. In one of the magnificent early renaissance-period wings, the ground floor houses the Deutsches Apothekenmuseum, a unique pharmaceutical museum. At cellar level the castle takes pride in its great cask which can hold 220,000 litres (48,00 gallons) of wine. It was built by order of the Elector Ottheinrich in an era when the Electors could claim a tithe of the annual wine-harvest of the Palatinate. Today it forms a scenic background for wine tasting.

Finally the great terrace of the castle, not far from the cellar of the wine cask, is a magnificent place for a stroll to admire the old town down below from many angles — and the Neckar valley beyond.

EXCURSIONS IN THE VICINITY OF HEIDELBERG

1 • No-one should omit to cross the river and take a walk along the Philosophenweg. From here is the classic photographic view of the city from the garden terraces on the slopes of the Heiligenberg hill. Cross the Neckar by the Theodor-Heuss-Brücke (north of the Bismarckplatz). The continuation north of the bridge is Brückenstrasse. The Philosophenweg goes off Brückenstrasse to the right and slopes up the north bank of the Neckar giving a series of beautiful 'bird's eye' views over the river, Heidelbergs's old town and Alte Brücke, and across to the castle framed in the greens of the wooded heights behind. Paths continue up to the top of the Heiligenberg (443m, 1,453ft) which makes about an hour's walk. In the ninth century monks from Lorsch built St Michael's Monastery there. Its church was later converted into an All Saints' Basilica, now a ruin, but which gave the hill its name 'Hill of the Saints'.

2 • The mountain railway from the Kornmarkt to Heidelberg Castle continues to the top of the Königstuhl (about a 20-minute journey). The Königstuhl (568m, 1,864ft) is one of the notable heights in the southern Odenwald. From it there are extensive and superb views over the Neckar valley. At the top is a television tower, and also a celestial observatory that can be visited on Thursday afternoons. There is also a Fairy Tale Garden for young children.

3 • During the summer a variety of boat-trips is available on the river Neckar, starting from the pier below the Stadthalle convention centre. They vary from a short local round-trip to a 3-hour excursion upstream by way of picturesque Neckargemünd to Neckarsteinach, with its scenic, ivy-covered castle ruins. No less than four castles were built here between 1100 and 1230, two of which have been restored while the ruins of the others complete a romantic back drop to the colourful old-world houses of the little town on the river bank.

Additional Information

Places of Interest

Heidelberg
Deutsches Apothekenmuseum
Im Heidelberger Schloss
Open: April-Oct 10am-5pm
weekdays; Sat, Sun 11am-5pm

Kurpfälzisches Museum
Hauptstr 97
Open: Tues-Sun 10am-1pm, 2-5pm

Observatory
Königstuhl
Open: Thurs 3-5pm
Reached by funicular railway,
which also goes to castle

Studentenkarzer
(Students' Prison)
Augustiner Gasse
Open: Mon-Sat 9am-5pm

Volkerkunde-Museum
(Museum of Ethnology)
Palais Weimar
Hauptstrasse 235
Open: Tues-Fri 3-5pm, Sun 1-5pm

Universitätsbibliothek
Plöck 107-109
Open: Mon-Sat 9am-7pm

Zoo
Tiergartenstr
Open: April to Sept 9am-7pm, Oct
to Mar 9am-5pm
☎ 48 00 41

Speyer
Historisches Museum der Pfalz
(Wine Museum)
Domplatz 4
☎ 06232 77131
Opening times depend on current
exhibitions

Kaiserdom
Domplatz
Open: Mon-Fri 8am-7pm, Sat 8am-
5pm, Sun 1.30-5pm. Mid-Oct to
March Mon-Fri 9-11.30am, 2-
4.30pm; Sat 9-11.30am, 1.30-4pm;
Sun 1.30-4.30pm

Altpörtel
Am Postplatz
Open: April-Oct daily 10am-
12noon, 2-4pm

Judenbad
Judenbadgasse
☎ 14395
Open: April-Oct daily 10am-
12noon, 2-5pm. Also by appointment

Gedächtniskirche
Bartholomäus Weltz-Platz
Open: Mon-Sat 10-12noon, 2-6pm,
Sun 2-6pm.

River Excursions

Heidelberg
Neckar boat-trips (from landing-
stage near Stadthalle) to Neckarsteinach
☎ 2 01 81 (or Hornung 48 00 64)

Hotels and Restaurants

Heidelberg
Hotel zum Ritter
Hauptstr 178
☎ 06221 24272
Famous hotel in historic renais-
sance house in Old Town.

Hotel-Garni am Schloss
Zwingerstr 20
Tel 06221 28255
Above Kornmarket Parkhaus,
terrace view of castle and old town.

Zum Roten Ochsen or Seppl
Hauptstrasse at Karlsplatz
Student taverns with food.

Speyer
Hotel Kurpfalz (garni)
Mühlturmstr 5
☎ 06232 24168
Buffet breakfast, otherwise no
restaurant. Parking

Tourist Information Centres

Heidelberg
Friedrich-Ebert Anlage 2
D-6900 Heidelberg
☎ 06221 10821

Speyer
Maximilianstrasse 11
D-6720 Speyer
☎ 06232 1 43 92

Rhine and Mosel: Fact File

Accommodation

A list of some 300 typical German hotels, as well as a list of the castle hotels which are a feature of the Rhineland, is available from the German National Tourist Office. Lists of the many privately run small hotels or inns (*Gasthöfe*) can be obtained by contacting regional or local tourist offices listed at the end if each chapter. Many local tourist offices will reserve rooms but not all will do this over the 'phone. When seeking accommodation look out for ar : *Zimmer Frei:* rooms to let, *Fremdenzimmer:* guest rooms, *Ferienwohnung*: holiday flat.

Camping

A free list of camp sites (*Campingplätze*) is available from the German National Tourist Office, regional and local tourist offices. There are some fairly expensive books listing camping stes published by the German Automobile Club (ADAC) and the Deutscher Camping Club available in larger bookshops and updated annually.

Most camping sites are open only between April to October, though near major cities or resorts with summer and winter seasons they remain open throughout the year.

Camping rough is illegal to protect the environment.

Hotels

The German Hotel Reservation System (ADZ), run by the German National Tourist Board (DZT) will book accommodation in all hotels, inns and boarding-houses. Contact:
DZT-Serviceabteilung ADZ
Corneliusstrasse 34
D-6000 Frankfurt am Main 1
☎ (069) 740767

Many resorts have an 'inclusive terms offer' (*Pauschal-Angebot*). For instance the 'Three Days in Heidelberg' run by the tourist office includes two nights with breakfast in a hotel, inn or pension, a bus tour of the city including the castle, a river cruise up the Neckar, a *table d'hote* dinner at a superior restaurant, another *table d'hote* meal in a historic student wine-pub, a free pass to the city's museums and 20 per cent discount at the theatre. The inclusive cost for two people is less than bed-and-breakfast alone at the same standard of accommodation.

Youth Hostels
German Youth Hostels are listed in the International Youth Hostels *Guide to Budget Accommodation Handbook, Volume 1, Europe and the Mediterranean.*
For further information contact:
Deutsches Jugendherbergswerk (DJH)
Hauptverband
Bismarckstrasse 8
Postfach 1455
D-4930 Detmold
☎ 05231/7401-0
Hostels in Germany are identified by a green triangle with the letters DJH.

Arrival and Customs

EEC nationals require no visa, only a valid passport. Holders of Australian, USA, Canadian, South African and New Zealand passports do not need a visa for stays of less than 3 months and provided they do not take up employment.

Customs Regulations
All personal belongings needed for a visit are duty-free.
Tobacco and alcoholic beverages are only duty-free for persons over 17 years of age and coffee only for persons over 15. In respect of goods bought in a tax/duty-free shop the regulations for imports from non-EEC countries apply.

Banks

Banks are usually open weekdays 8.30am-1pm and from

2.30-4pm (Thursday to 5.30pm), but close at weekends. Exchange offices at frontier crossings are normally open 6am-10pm.

The Deutsche Verkehrsbank has branches in railway stations of most main cities and are sometimes open all week and until quite late in the evening.

Business Hours

Shop opening times vary somewhat between the various Federal States. In general shops are open between 9am-6.30pm during the week, Saturdays until 2pm and they are closed Sundays.

On the first Saturday of every month, known as Langer Samstag, and in the 4 weeks before Christmas, shops may remain open until 6pm.

Museums and historic monuments are usually closed Mondays and admission charges for museums vary greatly. For the most part village churches are open during the day; if locked then check the notice board for the address of the Küster or whoever else might hold the key (Schlüssel). Large churches, cathedrals, and monasteries may have set opening times and if they are not pinned up by the main entrance then inquire at the tourist office. Visitors should refrain from taking photos during services; especially with a flash. At some of the more important places there are often booklets or leaflets available in English.

Chemists

The Apotheke (chemist's or pharmacist's shop) is open during normal business hours. Usually clearly visible at the shop front are details of which chemist is on night or Sunday duty (Apothekennotdienst or simply Notdienst). This information is also found in the local newspapers.

Medicines are only available on doctor's prescription from the chemist. No prescription is necessary for aspirins and other mild medicaments. A Drogerie (drug store) sells things like insect repellents, vitamin tablets etc.

Climate

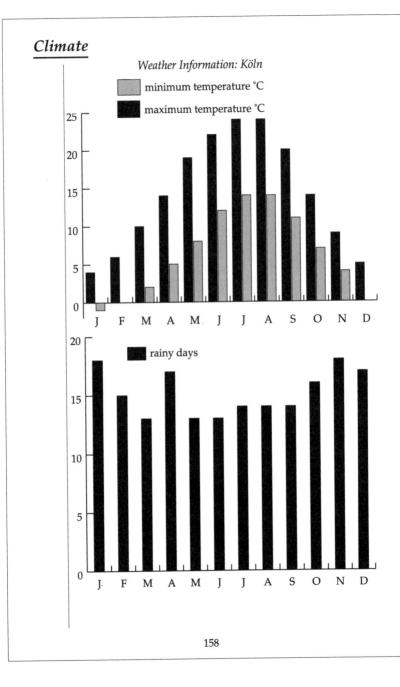

Weather Information: Köln

minimum temperature °C
maximum temperature °C

rainy days

Consulates

The main German consulates are:

CANADA
German Consulate General
77 Admiral Road
Toronto
Ontario M5R 2L4
☎ (416) 925-2813

USA
German Consulate General
New York
NY
460 Park Ave
☎ (212) 308-8700

UK
German Consulate General
16 Eglinton Crescent
Edinburgh EH 12 5D9
☎ (031) 337 23 23

The main consulates in Germany are:

CANADA
Consulate
Godesberger Allee 119
5300 Bonn 2
☎ (0228) 8100630

UK
General Consulate
Triton House
Bockenheimer Landstrasse 42
6000 Frankfurt am Main
☎ (069) 1700020

Currency and Credit Cards

The German unit of currency is the Deutsche Mark (DM). 100 Pfennigs (Pf) = 1DM. It is freely convertible ie, it can be exchanged for any foreign currency at the going rate. You can bring as much currency as you wish into Germany.

The Deutsche Mark comes in **notes** of DM10, DM20, DM50, DM100, DM200, DM500 and DM1,000; **coins** of DM0.01 (one pfennig), DM0.02, DM0.05, DM0.10, DM0.20, DM0.50, DM1, DM2 and DM5.

Credit cards are not so widely accepted as in some other countries, especially outside large cities and major tourist centres. In smaller towns banks only accept American Express or Euro-Cards.

All banks exchange traveller's cheques. If the cheques are in Deutschmarks the full face value will be given. If they are in a foreign currency the bank will make a service charge of around 2 per cent.

Eurocheques, together with a cheque card, are used like ordinary domestic cheques and must be made out in the local currency. Eurocheques can be used for all business transactions but petrol stations make a small additional charge. These cheques can only be cashed up to a value of 400DM per transaction. Scottish bank notes are not accepted for exchange nor are foreign coins.

Bureaux de change: at airports, main railway stations and border crossings. Open: usually 6am-10pm.

The Deutsches Verkehrsbank will give a cash advance against major credit cards, subject to a DM100 minimum.

Disabled Facilities

Facilities for the disabled are fairly good in Germany. Facilities are usually indicated by the blue pictogram of a person in a wheelchair. Most motorway service stops have toilet facilities for the handicapped and there are usually reserved parking places for people in wheelchairs in multi-storey car parks and elsewhere. Most important museums and public buildings are accessible for the handicapped. Town guides for the handicapped are available (free) at tourist offices in major cities and are mostly bilingual.

The information from some of the following addresses may only be in German:

Infozentrale für Behinderte
(Information Centre for the Disabled)
8000 Munich
☎ (089) 21171

Club der Behinderten und ihrer Freunde
Eupenerstrasse 5
D-6500 Mainz
☎ (06131) 225514
Very good for general information on travel etc, but when writing be prepared to allow for a bit of time before getting an answer (this organisation is run on a voluntary basis).

Reisebüro für Behinderte BTS
Behinderten Touristic Service
(Travel Agent for the Disabled)
D-6700 Ludwigshafen/Rhein

Handicapped Reisen
Am Markt 33
5300 Bonn 1

Behindertenreisen
Jahn Reisen
(Travel company)
Elsenheimer Strasse 61
D-8000 Munich 21

Zentrale Verkaufsleitung der Deutschen Bundesbahn
(Kontaktstelle für Behindertenfragen)
Rhabanusstrasse 3
D-6500 Mainz
☎ (06131) 1552 16
Contact the above address for information about the
facilities offered by German Federal Railways for the
handicapped. They put out the *Reiseführer für unsere
behinderten Fahrgäste* (*Travel Guide for Disabled Passengers* —
partly in English). It is available at train stations, DB
(Federal Rail) agencies and DER travel bureaux.

Gesellschaft für Nebenbetriebe der Bundesautobahn (GfN)
Poppelsdorfer Allee 24
D-5300 Bonn 1
☎ (0228) 7090
For the pamphlet *Autobahn-Service für Behinderte* (*Motor-
way-Service for the Disabled*).

Electricity

Electricity operates at 220 volts AC 50 Hertz. Round ended,
two pronged continental adaptors are needed for UK/USA
appliances. Note that the adaptor should be constructed so as
to fit into recessed sockets.

Embassies

The main embassies in Germany are:

Australia
2 Godesberger Allee 107
5300 Bonn
☎ (0228) 8103-0

Canada
Friedrich Wilhelm Strasse 18
5300 Bonn
☎ (0228) 231061

UK
1 Friedrich Ebert Allee 77
5300 Bonn
☎ (0228) 234061

Other foreign embassies in
Germany are listed in the
telephone book under
Botschaften.

Main German embassies are:

Australia
119 Empire Circuit
Yarralumla, ACT 2600
Canberra
☎ (062) 701911

UK
23 Belgrave Square
London
SW1X 8PZ
☎ 071 2355033

Canada
1 Waverley Street
Ottawa, Ontario K2P OT8
☎ (613) 232-1101

USA
4645 Reservoir Road NW
Washington DC
☎ (202) 298-4000

New Zealand
90-2 Hobson Street
Thornton, Wellington
☎ 85 02 89

Festivals

There are many more festivals and local events than can be
listed here. A calendar of events is obtainable from the
National Tourist Office or at regional and local tourist offices.

Aachen
International Tournament
of Horse-jumping; September Crafts Market

Adenau
International motor racing
at nearby Nurburgring

Andernach
Andernacher Kirmes;
Weinlesefest (Wine Harvest
Festival)

Bad Ems
Blumencorso last Sunday

in August; Whitsun
Fireworks; Rowing Regatta

Bad Kreuznach
Jahrmark on third weekend
in August; Brunnen-fest
first weekend in June

Bernkastel-Kues
Mittelmosel Weinfest first
weekend in September

Bingen
'Magic Rhine in Flames'
first Saturday in July

Bonn
Triennial Beethoven Festival

Braubach
Festival of Roses second
weekend in June; 'Rhine
Aflame' second weekend in
August

Koblenz
'Rhine in Flames' second
Saturday in August

Köln
Winter Carnival Season;
Rhine regatta early June

Mainz
Wine Market August-
September; Carnival in
early season

Monschau
Folk music week in
August; Fest & Kirmes in
September; Art Craft
Market in mid-September

Nierstein
Weinfest (several); Day of
Open Wine Cellars third
weekend in September

Rüdesheim
Magic Rhine in Flames
third Saturday in September

St Goar
Rhine in Flames third
Saturday in September

St Goarshausen
Rhine in Flames third
Saturday in September

Traben-Trabach
Several festivals

Wiesbaden
Morning Concerts in Kur-
haus rotunda

Worms
Backfischfest last weekend
in August to first weekend
in September

Food and Drink

In Germany a *Restaurant* often implies some degree of formality, while a *Gaststätte* is less formal. A *Café* will invariably
serve meals; snack bars are indicated by an *Imbiss* or *Schnell
Imbiss* sign, although readily recognised anyway. *Speise(n)*
indicates that meals are available. A menu is *a Speise-karte*,
while a *Menü* indicates a set meal.

The cuisine of the Rhine and Mosel region is good and
varied. Pork (*Schweinfleisch*) is the most common meat, prepared as the popular *Schnitzel* or in a variety of other ways:
Pfannengerichte (fried dishes), grills, roasts and casseroles.
Venison is common in the uplands, either as cuts from the
saddle (*Rehrücken*) or from the haunch (*Reh-keule*). A regional
meat dish is *Sauerbraten*, a pickled beef stew served with
greens or pickled cabbage (*Sauerkraut*). *Eisbein* is a giant-

sized hot dish of picled pork-knuckle with accompaniments.

In restaurants *offene Wein*, 'open' or 'carafe' wine, is usually of good quality and of local origin and served in a large (0.2 litre) Römer glass or an individual 0.25 litre earthenware carafe with a smaller drinking glass. Wine can be *trocken*: dry, *halb-trocken*: fairly dry, or *lieblich*: smooth and mild.

Health Insurance

Visitors from the UK are covered by reciprocal agreements when in Germany. They require an E111 form which can be obtained from their local post office or DHSS office. Nationals of other countries should ensure that they have adequate medical cover before departing.

Language

Although English is quite widely spoken it is a good idea to get a decent phrase book such as *Berlitz Language Guide: German for Travellers* or *Language Guide Germany* by Polyglott. Even mastery of the very simplest phrases produces a positive response. Note that 'ß' is sometimes used in German to represent a double 's'. What follows is a list of names frequently used in the text and encountered when touring.

Abtei — abbey
Altstadt — old quarter of town
Apotheke — chemist, pharmacist
Autobahn (A-) — motorway
Bad — spa
Berg — mountain
Bundesstrasse (B-) — Federal road
Dom — cathedral
Freibad — outdoor swimming pool
Fremdenverkehrsamt/Verkehrsamt — tourist office
Gaststätte — restaurant
Gondelbahn — cable railway
Hallenbad — indoor swimming pool
Hauptbahnhof — main railway station
Heimatmuseum — local museum
Kirche — church
Kloster — monastery, nunnery or convent

Marktplatz — market square
Münster — minster
Naturlehrpfad — nature trail
Naturschutzgebiet — nature reserve
Pkw — parking space for private cars (not trucks, buses)
Rathaus — town hall
See — lake
Seilbahn — cable railway
Tal — valley
Tierpark — zoo
Tor — gate
Veste — fortress
Wanderparkplatz — car park situated near walking area
Wallfahrtskirche — pilgrimage church
Weinlehpfad — wine instruction trail
Weinprobe — wine tasting

Maps

Maps to the scale of 1:700,000 or 1:800,000 give a good overall view, while including enough detail to make following the routes described relatively easy. Excellent choices obtainable in Germany are *Deutschland 1:800,000* in the *Euro-Länderkarte* series. For more detailed exploration of the Rhine-Mosel region individual sheets on a scale of 1:200,000 or 1:300,000 are ideal. Maps to similar scales are published by the fuel companies and are available at most filling stations. This guide was compiled using the *Euro-Regionalkarte* 1:300,000 'Hessen Rheinland-Pfalz Saarland' (Bundesrepublik Deutschland 3) published by RV Verlag (available in Britain and Germany). Michelin's 'Germany' map 412 covering Nordrhein-Westfalen as well as Rheinland-Pfalz, Hessen and Saarland to a scale of 1:400,000 indicates road distances clearly and has an index of place names.

Measurements

The metric system is used in Germany.
1 kilogram (1,000 grams) = 2.2lb
1 litre = $1^3/_4$ pints, 4.5 litres = 1 gallon
1 kilometre = 0.62 miles (10km = approximately 6 miles).

Medical Treatment

Doctors' (*Arzt*) and Dentists' (*Zahnarzt*) consulting hours are normally 10am-12noon and 4-6pm, except Wednesdays, Saturdays and Sundays. Note that in some cases they could be open earlier and longer — it depends on the doctor. To call an ambulance dial 110.

Post Offices

Post Offices (*die Post* or *Postamt*) are usually open Monday to Friday 8am-6pm, Saturdays 8am-12noon. At railway stations in larger cities they are open during the week until late in the evening. Post offices can also change currency.

Public Holidays

1 January *Neujahr* (New Year's Day)
6 January *Heilige Drei Könige* (Epiphany)
Karfreitag (Good Friday)
Ostermontag (Easter Monday)
1 May *Tag der Arbeit* (May Day, Labour Day)
Pfingstmontag (Whit Monday)
Fronleichnam (Corpus Christi. In areas with mainly
    Catholic population)
15 August *Mariae Himmelfahrt* (Assumption of Mary. In
    areas with mainly Catholic population)
3 October *Tag der deutschen Einheit* (Day of German Unity)
1 November *Allerheiligen* (All Saints Day. In Rhineland-
    Palatinate)
Buss- und Bettag (Repentence Day. In all Federal States)
Weihnachten (Christmas)

Public Transport

Bus services run jointly by the railway and postal authorities, as well as by other operators, supplement the rail network. The Europa-Bus Service runs tours along particularly interesting routes for visitors. Reservations contact:
Deutsche Touring GmbH
Am Römerhof 17
D-6000 Frankfurt am Main

To make reservations from overseas contact your local travel agent, offices of the Deutsche Touring GmbH or a Europa-Bus agent.

Smoking

Some restaurants have non-smoking *(Nichtraucher)* sections. The car hire firm Inter Rent/Europcar offers a 'No-Smoking' car which is available at all German airports.

Sports and Pastimes

Angling

Permits are required for fishing in Germany.

1. National permit — obtainable from appropriate district administration *(Landratsamt)* or town council *(Stadtverwaltung — Ordnungsamt)*.
2. Permits from the fishing water owner or lease-holder *(Fischwasserbesitzer* or *Fischwasserpächter)*. Tourist offices should be able to help visitors with this.

Stocks of fish to be found in Germany include carp, pike, perch, pike-perch, sheat-fish, eels, bream, barbel, chub, rudd, trout, char, and salmon.

Details of facilities, etc, can be obtained from:

Verband Deutscher Sportfischer (VDSF)
Bahnhofstrasse 37
D-6050 Offenbach

Walking

Walking is one of Germany's great national pastimes. The number and length of waymarked trails is immense. For the motorist the numerous *Wanderparkplätze* (walkers' car parks) are ideal. They are almost always marked by the pictogram of a couple walking, are free, and there is usually an information board with a map, including length and duration of the walks. These trails or *Wanderwege* are mostly of a circular nature and might take from an hour to a full day at the most. For longer walks a map *(Wanderkarte)* showing the various trails is recommended, as the many different symbols used along some trails can get confusing. The best scales are from 1:75,000/1:50,000 for covering a fairly large area and 1:25,000 for more detail. Walking guides such as the *Kompass Wander-führer* are useful for German speaking visitors as they give very detailed descriptions of walks and cover virtually all Germany. For further information contact:

Europäische Wandervereinigung/Verband Deutscher Gebirgs-und Wandervereine, Reichsstrasse 4
6600 Saarbrücken, ☎ (0681) 390070

There are desingated footpaths along the whole length of the Mosel, on both banks, that include river banks, hillsides, vineyards, panoramic viewpoints and castles. Similar marked trails exist in the Rhine valley, eg the *Loreley Valley Trail* and the *Rheingau Valley Trail*. Brochures are available from local tourist offices.

WANDERN OHNE GEPÄCK (WALKING WITHOUT LUGGAGE)

This service involves a hike along a specific route where certain *Gasthöfe* not only offer accommodation but also transfer luggage to the next *Gasthof* on the route. Organised tours of this type — where hotel reservations, etc, are all taken care of — often have to be booked at least 3 weeks in advance and can be quite cheap if undertaken in spring or autumn. It is often much more comfortable at this time of the year anyway.

Wandern ohne Gepäck and *Radeln ohne Gepäck* (Cycling without Luggage) are organised on a regional and local (not national) basis. If DER travel offices or German National Tourist Offices overseas cannot provide sufficient information then it is best to write to the regional tourist offices. They should be able to provide specific information on the nature of the walk — pamphlets with route descriptions, sometimes route maps and costs. To be sure of a reply it is best to include an International Reply Coupon. Some tourist offices will help visitors organise such a walk within their region and reserve rooms in the various *Gasthöfe*. Note that individual hikers usually have to pay a bit more for the transport of their luggage than groups — in some cases two people already qualify as a group.

The Verband Deutscher Gebirgs and Wandervereine (see address above) also offers information on organised walks (with and without backpack) and cycling tours (*Rad-Wanderung*). They must have an International Reply Coupon for a reply.

A favourite area for *Wandern ohne Gepäck* is the Hunsrück:
One route is known as *Auf Schusters Rappen im Land des Blauen
Löwen* (On Shank's Pony through the land of the Blue Lion)
Length: the daily stages are between 15 & 25km (9 &15 miles)
Route: Idar-Oberstein — Stipshausen — Idar-Oberstein
Time: 7 days (maps provided)
Information on this walk and also riding tours, cycling
tours and covered waggon safari from:
Fremdenverkehrsamt Idar-Oberstein
Postfach 01 1480
D-6580 Idar-Oberstein
☎ (06781) 27025

Taxis

Fares are made up of a basic flat rate plus a charge per
kilometre, and vary from place to place. Surcharges for
luggage also vary. Meters are obligatory.

Telephones

In the main post offices you can use the direct phone service.
Ask at the counter marked *Ferngespräche* for a phone booth.
You pay at the counter when you have finished your phone
call. This is much more convenient than queuing for a pay
phone and saves having to find change.

Every telephone booth has a local directory. Phone books
covering all Germany are found in the post offices. Local and
national calls may be made from all post offices and coin/
card-operated phone booths. Unit fees for calls from hotels
are about twice as expensive as the standard call units.
International calls can be made from post offices and phone
booths with a phone marked *Auslandsgespräche*.

Coins that can be used in a phone booth are: 10 Pfennig,
1DM, 5DM. A much more comfortable way of telephoning is
with a Telefonkarte. These cards are available at post offices
and solve the problem of small change. Telephone booths
which accept these cards are usually marked *Kartentelefon* —
they are becoming more widespread but may not yet exist in
smaller towns or villages.

You can only reverse charges (*R-Gespräch*, ring collect) to the USA. To do this look up the number of the international *Fernamt* under the heading *Telefon-Sonderdienste* in the telephone book. This number is usually 0010 but it can vary from region to region. The person at reception will then give further details. You cannot ring collect within Germany.

Instructions on how to use payphones are written in English in phone booths for international calls. Otherwise lift the receiver, insert the coins and dial the number. A meter shows how much credit is left.

For international directory inquiries dial 0 01 18. This number will also help if you have language difficulties in finding a number in an emergency.

Emergency Numbers
Police and accidents 110. Fire brigade 112
National directory inquiries dial 11 88 or 0 11 88

Main international direct dialling codes are:
Australia 00 61
Britain 0044
Irish Republic 00 353
New Zealand 00 64
USA and Canada 00 1
Telephone call rates are cheaper after 8pm and at weekends. This does not apply to calls outside Germany.

When calling from Germany after dialling the national code omit the first zero of the number you are ringing.

Tipping

Not a must but usual for good service. Small sums are rounded up, sums over 100DM might include a tip of 2DM.

Tourist Offices

The main German National Tourist Offices are:

Australia
Lufthansa House
12th Floor
143 Macquarie Street
Sydney 2000
☎ (02) 221-1008

Canada
175 Bloor Street East
North Tower, 6th Floor
Toronto
Ontario M4 W3R8
☎ (416) 968-1570

Box 417
2 Fundy
Place Bonaventure
Montreal H5A 1B8
☎ (514) 878-9885

Germany
Deutsche Zentrale für
    Tourismus e.V. (DZT)
Beethovenstrasse 69
6000 Frankfurt am Main
☎ (069) 7572-0

Deutsche Fremden-
    verkehrsverband
Niebuhrstrasse 16b
5300 Bonn 1
☎ (0228) 214071-72

USA
444 South Flower Street
Suite 2230
Los Angeles
CA 90071
☎ (213) 688-7332

747 Third Avenue
33rd Floor
New York
NY 10017
☎ (212) 308-3300

UK
Nightingale House
65 Curzon Street
London W1Y 7PE
☎ (041) 4953990

Regional Tourist Offices in Germany are:

For the State of Rheinland-
Pfalz:
Fremdenenverkehrsverband
    Rheinland Pfalz
Postfach 1420
D-5400 Koblenz
☎ 0261 31079

For the State of Hessen:
Hessiche Landeszentrale
    für Fremdenverkehr
Abraham Lincoln-Str 38-42
D-6200 Wiesbaden
☎ 06121 7 37 25

For Northern Rheinland:
LVV Rheinland
Rheinallee 69
D-5300 Bonn 2
☎ 0228 362921

Travel

By Air
Intercontinental flights are mostly catered for by Frankfurt
Airport, which has its own railway station directly beneath
the terminal building with a link with the Frankfurt main
railway station by a 10-minute S-Bahn (suburban) service.
There is also a S-Bahn service to Mainz and Wiesbaden from
the airport. There are direct InterCity services hourly to and

from Koblenz (with Trier connection), Bonn and Cologne. Trains run to Frankfurt's main railway station at 10 minute intervals; length of journey is around 11 minutes.

From European countries there are flights to Köln/Bonn Airport with a bus link to the main railway station at Köln (20 minutes) and Bonn (30 minutes).

Lufthansa German Airlines link more than 1,000 cities throughout the world with Germany. Many other airlines also have direct services:

Lufthansa Offices
Canada
55 Yonge Street
Toronto, Ontario M5E IJ4
☎ (416) 3 60-36 00
Reservations:
☎ (414) 2 83-77 00
(also in Montreal, Ottawa, Calgary and Vancouver)

Germany
Deutsche Lufthansa AG
Von-Gablenz-Strasse 2-6,
D-5000 Köln 21

UK
23-26 Piccadilly
London W1V 0EJ
(also in Birmingham, Bristol, Glasgow, and Manchester)

USA
680 Fifth Avenue
New York NY 10019
☎ (212) 357-8400
(and many other American cities)

Domestic Air Services
There are regular flight connections between all German airports. As a supplementary service to the existing flight schedule the Lufthansa Airport Express Train links the airports of Cologne, Bonn and Frankfurt.

All airports are linked to their local urban transport network. Some even have their own shuttle service — eg bus or direct trains to the city centre. There are DB (German Rail) offices at all airports.

River Cruises
The Köln-Düsseldorfer (KD) German Rhine Line has a fleet of day-excursion vessels operating between Köln and Mainz, as well as a fleet of modern 'hotel-ships' which cruise the Rhine between Nijmegen in Holland and Basel in Switzerland. There are cruises from Frankfurt-am-Main to Koblenz then along the Mosel to Trier; from Trier to Koblenz and then Köln; from Köln to Mainz and then to Frankfurt.

KD Deutsche Rheinschiffahrt AG
Frankenwerft 15, D-5000 Köln 1
☎ 0221 2088-318

Their agents overseas are:

Canada
KD German Rhine Line Representatives
Holiday House
25 Adelaide St East
Toronto, Ontario M5C 1H7
or
Holiday House
2100 Drummond Street
Suite 536
Montreal PQ
H3G 1X1

UK
G A Clubb Rhine Cruise
  Agency Ltd
80-1 St Martin's Lane
London WC2

USA
KD German Rhine Line
170 Hamilton Avenue
White Plains NY 10601
☎ (914) 948-3600
or
323 Geary Street
San Francisco CA 94102
☎ (415) 392-8817

Swan-Hellenic Cruises have cruises, with a specialist guest-lecturer, on the Rhine from Holland to Basel, with a trip along the Mosel to Cochem and a coach excursion to Trier.

Swan-Hellenic Cruises
77 New Oxford Street
London WC1A 1PP
☎ 071 831 1616

For exact details about short excursions inquire at the local tourist offices. Information about longer cruises on the Rhine should be available at most travel agents or from the various German National Tourist Offices overseas.

Cycling

Cycling is very popular, designated cycle paths are common and in the Rhine gorge there are riverside cycle paths.

From April to October bicycles can be hired at many railway stations in Germany (includeing most in the Rhineland) and can be returned to any other station that offers this service. For a list of these stations inquire at a main railway station in one of the larger cities. Tourist offices have lists of other places hiring out bicycles and sometimes they even have maps. Detailed *Radwanderkarten* (maps showing cycling routes) are available at many bookshops. If you are in an area without a cycle hire station look in a phone book under *Fahrradverleih* to find addresses of local bike rental outlets.

To take your bike on a train you need to purchase a 'bicycle ticket' or *Fahrrad-Karte*. You have to take the bike to the luggage carriage yourself. For further information contact:
Bund Deutscher Radfahrer
Otto-Fleck-Schneise 4
D-6000 Frankfurt 71
☎ (069) 678 92 22

In the MiddleMosel where there are no riverside railways the bus service on the Trier-Bernkastel-Bullay route has special buses for carrying cycles.
Timetables for these *Radel-Bus* routes are issued by
Mosel-Omnibusverkehr
Schönbornstrasse 7
D-5500 Trier

Road Travel

A safe way of covering against risks to vehicle or passengersis to have an insurance package such as the Automobile Association's 'Five Star Service' for motoring holidays abroad. Your insurance company should be contacted at least a month before to go for advice on adequacy of cover. An insurance Green Card is recommended.

Breakdown

German motoring organisations are the Allgeiner Deutscher Automobil Club (ADAC) and the Automobilclub von Deutschland (AvD). They operate road patrols and will help members of foreign organisations. A 24-hour breakdown service exists in most large cities; first dial the area code and then 19211. On motorways and some main roads help can be called from one of the orange emergency telephones. Motorway telephones are clearly indicated and may be used by the motorist in distress to communicate with the police who will, inform the ADAC patrol. Emergency telephones are now gradually being installed on other main roads.

ADAC	AvD
Am Westpark 8	Lyonner Strasse 16
D-8000 Munich 70	D-6000 Frankfurt-Niederrad
☎ (089) 76 76-0	

The brochure *Autobahn Service* contains detailed information about motorway petrol stations, service areas and motels. It is available from all tourist offices.

Parking

Free parking is rare in German towns and cities. Time is saved by going direct to a multi-storey car park (*Parkhaus*). They are always clearly signposted by a 'P' with an inverted 'v' top. Parking is forbidden on main roads or those with fast moving traffic, on or near tram lines, near bus or tram stops, traffic lights, taxi ranks and intersections. It is also forbidden to park on the 'wrong' side of the road, except in one-way streets.

The hassles of driving into many cities can be avoided by using the 'P+R' (Park and Ride) system; a large car park outside the city centre from where regular trains or buses depart for the inner-city. The large car parks are free of charge. The bus/train that travels a short distance into the inner-city is quite modest in price compared to the cost of a multi-storey car park. Not every city, however, offers this service. In order to discourage parking in inner-cities parking meters sometimes only have a duration of thirty minutes. Some of the larger towns, especially spas, offer free parking outside the town centre but still within walking distance.

Driving Regulations

UK, American and Canadian citizens may drive for up to 1 year in Germany using a valid national driving licences or an international driver's licence. National or international vehicle registration papers should also be carried.

Third party insurance is compulsory in Germany and foreign visitors, other than nationals of EEC countries, must have an international insurance certificate (Green Card) or take out third party insurance at the border. This is obtainable for 15 days or 1 month. On expiring this temporary insurance can be extended — as can the Green Card — at any office of the Automobile Association (ADAC).

Germans drive on the right-hand side of the road. Speed limits are as follows: in towns and villages 50km (31mph); outside built up areas 100km (62mph); on motorways 130km (81mph) is recommended. These speeds are not indicated by signs but variations from them are shown in km per hour. At the entrance to a town or village a rectangular yellow sign bearing the place name denotes the start of a built up area and a similar sign with a diagonal stripe indicates its end. Place names on a green sign do not constitute a speed restriction.

Other than on minor roads in rural areas, priority is always indicated on signs approaching a junction. Traffic on a *Bundesstrasse* (state main road) always has priority. *Bundesstrassen* are recognised by a small rectangular yellow plate bearing the road number. Priority is shown elsewhere by a yellow square with white border set on its corner while the same sign with diagonal black line indicates the end of priority. Standard 'Give Way' or 'Stop' signs will be found on converging roads.

The German police are very strict on tyre condition and a vehicle found with less than 2mm tread depth over the whole surface will not be allowed to proceed until the tyres have been replaced.

Warning triangles are compulsory and must be placed 100m (109yd) behind a broken down vehicle and 200m (219yd) on an *Autobahn*.

Seat belts are compulsory for those riding in the front seat and children under 12 years must sit in the back. There are on-the-spot fines for speeding and other offences, including running out of fuel on an *Autobahn*.

Blood alcohol levels must not exceed 0.8 per mille (80mg/100ml). If caught drinking and driving the penalties are stiff.

Fuel
Though leaded fuel is available everywhere the trend is to unleaded (*Bleifrei*) — this is always indicated on the pumps, so check first! Note that although Super grade is available in leaded (*Verbleiter*) form, normal grade fuel (*Benzin*) is only available in unleaded form.

Useful Road Signs

Ausfahrt — Exit from motorway or dual carriageway
Bankett nicht befahrbar — Soft verges
Einbahnstrasse — One-way street
Einordnen — Get in lane
Freie Fahrt — End of restrictions, usually after passing
   roadworks
Gegenverkehr — Oncoming traffic
Glatteisgefahr — Danger of icy road
Langsam fahren — Drive slowly
Rollsplit — Loose clippings
Stau — Traffic jam ahead
Umleitung (on yellow arrow) — Traffic diversion
Links/Rechts fahren — Drive on the left/right

Vehicle Lights

Left-dipping headlights must be adjusted to dip to the right. Cars may not be driven on sidelights and headlights must be used, even during daylight hours, if visibility is impaired by fog, snow, rain, etc. Rear fog lights may be used if visibility is less than 50m (160ft) but not in built-up areas.

Car Hire (*Autovermietung*)

This is available at most airports and major train stations. Generally you have to be 21 years old to hire a car. For small models (VW Polo, VW Golf) 19 years is accepted at InterRent/Europcar; for a big Mercedes you must be at least 25 years old. A valid national driving licence held for at least 1 year is required. Major credit cards and cash are accepted. The following companies have a central reservation service (the calls are at local rates throughout Germany):

Avis ☎ (0130) 7733

Hertz ☎ (0130) 2121 (calls free)

InterRent ☎ (0130) 2211 and 3151

Sixt/Budget ☎ (0130) 3366

Head Offices

ai/Ansa International Rent-a-Car
Savignystrasse 71
D-6000 Frankfurt am Main 1
☎ (0469) 75 61 00-20

Avis Autovermietung
Eschersheimer Landstrasse 55
D-6000 Frankfurt am Main 1
☎ (069) 15 37-0

Europcar Autovermietung
Frankfurter Ring 243
D-8000 Munich 40
☎ (089) 3 23 09-0

Hertz Autovermietung
Schwalbacher Strasse 47-49
6000 Frankfurt am Main 1
☎ (069) 75850

Inter Rent Autovermietung
Tangstedter Landstrasse 81
D-2000 Hamburg 62
☎ (040) 52 01 80

Sixt/Budget Rent-a-Car
Dr-Carl-von-Linde-Strasse 2
D-8023 Pullach
☎ (089) 79 10 71

Mitfahrzentrale

This is an organised alternative to hitch-hiking for young people. By going to one of the *Mitfahr* travel offices in most large cities it is possible to get lifts with private motorists. A modest fee is payable to the office for booking rides and they also advise on the maximum fee to be paid to drivers. There is a safety factor in this system as all drivers have to notify agencies of their addresses and car registration numbers. Female passengers can, if they wish, choose female drivers.

Mitfahrzentrale (MFZ)
Gutleutstrasse 125
6000 Frankfurt am Main 1
☎ (069) 230291

By Sea

Motorists travelling from Scotland, northern England or the Midlands may find the North Sea Ferries services from Hull to Rotterdam or Zeebrugge (14 hours) convenient. On the east coast there are the shorter Felixstowe to Zeebrugge and Harwich to the Hook of Holland routes (7-8 hours), operated by P&O Ferries and Sealink respectively. South of the Thames overnight crossings can be made from Sheerness to Vlissingen (Flushing, around 8 hours) with Olau Lines and from Ramsgate to Dunkirk with Sally Viking. There are day and night crossings from Folkestone or Dover to Ostend and Zeebrugge with P&O Ferries taking about 4 hours. Finally there are many sailings on the short sea route from Dover to Calais with P&O Ferries.

The majority of rail travellers will no doubt go via London and cross from Harwich to the Hook of Holland or from Dover to Ostend. If overnight sailings are used the Rhine and Mosel can be reached in the course of a day. It is 181 miles

from Rotterdam to Köln and 283 miles from Rotterdam to
Rüdesheim.

North Sea Ferries
King George Dock
Hedon Road
Hull HU9 5QA
☎ 0482 77177

Car Ferry Terminal
The Docks
 Felixstowe
Suffolk IP11 8TB
☎ (0394) 604802

Sally Line
Argyle Centre
York Street
Ramsgate CT11 9DS
☎ (0843) 595566

The Continental Ferry Port
Mile End
Portsmouth
Hampshire PO2 8QW
☎ (0705) 827677

Münchener Strasse 48
D-6000 Frankfurt am Main 1
☎ (069) 250197 or 236798

Graf-Adolf-Strasse 41
D-4000 Düsseldorf 1
☎ (0211) 387060

P&O European Ferries
Russell Street
Dover CT16 1QB
☎ (0304) 203388

By Train

The resorts on the Rhine are well served by German Rail
(*Deutsche Bundesbahn* or DB). Main lines operate on both
banks of the Rhine and through fares are available to most
Rhine destinations from London by way of Dover-Ostend
and Harwich-Hook of Holland. The journey can be broken at
some thirty towns and villages between Köln and Mainz to
join a KD German Rhine Line ship for a day-long river cruise,
for payment of a small supplement.

A good way to explore Germany is by using a German Rail
Pass, available exclusively to visitors from abroad and can
only be bought outside Germany. Regional Pass 111 Köln/
Mainz/Rhine-Mosel — which actually extends from Düsseldorf to Heidelberg, including Frankfurt — covers the whole
area of this guide and more besides. Regional Passes are only
available to visitors from Great Britain and Ireland and
cannot be obtained in Germany. A passport (a similar document) must be produced when purchasing. Regional passes
have an overall validity of 21 days, within which unlimited

travel is possible on five or ten days at the holder's choice. Full details are available from German Rail Distribution, 18 Chertsey Road, Woking, Surrey GU21 5AB; from a recommended German Rail agent, eg The European Rail Office of American Express Europe Ltd, London; DER Travel Service, London; or from a good travel agent.

You can plan your route by train using the new *Thomas Cook Germany Timetable* which contains a 100-page summary of rail services to and within all of the unified Germany.

Most trains have first and second class compartments, as well as smoking/non-smoking compartments (*Raucher/ Nichtraucher*). All have toilets (WC). Trains in Germany are not particularly cheap but there are many special reduced fares. The booklet *Happy Days in Germany* available from tourist offices has details of several bargain rail tickets.

Children up to 4 years of age travel free of charge. Those between the ages of 4 and 11 and younger children occupying a sleeping-car berth or couchette pay half fare only and half the InterCity and EuroCity train supplements.

Nah-Schnellverkehrszug (local train): stops nearly everywhere, therefore comparatively slow. Good for visiting smaller towns and villages.

Eilzug (express): faster than latter. Stops at bigger stations.

D-Zug/FD-Zug/Interregio (through-trains): even faster. Only stops at larger towns or cities. For journeys under 50km (31 miles) an additional 3DM has to be paid. The Interregio train is a bit more comfortable than the D/FD-Zug.

Intercity/Eurocity: fastest of the lot and most comfortable. Travel only between the main cities. Additional 6DM has to be paid on top of fare. Only worthwhile for long distances and for people who are really in a hurry.

Autoreisezug (Motorail): German Federal Rail's service links up with the European network. By night passengers travel in sleeping-cars or couchettes and by day in first class carriages. Cars are carried on the same train. An overall charge is made for car and driver, with reduced rates for accompanying passengers. Destinations in Germany can be reached by Motorail from Holland, Belgium and France.

Luggage Services

Luggage services are provided by German Federal Rail .

Door to door luggage service (Haus-und-Gepäckservice)
Contact the railway station (ask for the *Gepäckannahmestelle*) from where you plan to depart a few days before you leave. Your luggage will be collected and delivered to you destination hotel.

Porter and taxi service (Gepäckträgerservice und Taxiservice)
A porter wearing a green jacket with the badge 'DB Gepäckträger-Service' carries hand-luggage from and to the platform or from platform to platform.

If a taxi is also required the taxi driver will collect passengers and their hand-luggage direct from the train and drive them to their hotel. Just book the *Gepäckträgerservice* beforehand.

For further information about rail tours etc contact:

Canada
DER Travel Service Ltd
1290 Bay Street
Toronto
Ontario M5R 2C3
☎ (416) 968-3272

Germany
Deutsches Reisebüro GmbH
Eschersheimer Landstrasse
  25-27
Postfach 100701
D-6000 Frankfurt (Main)
☎ (069) 1566-289 or 345

Deutsche Bundesbahn
Rhabanusstrasse 3
D-6500 Mainz

UK
DER Travel Service
18 Conduit Street
London W1R 9TD
☎ 071 4081111

German Rail
Suite 118, Hudson's Place
Victoria Station
London SW1V 1JL
(no personal callers)

USA
DER Travel Service Inc
230 Park Avenue
Suite 1511
New York

New World Travel Inc
747 Third Avenue
18th Floor
New York NY 10017
☎ (21) 308-3100

German Rail
One Hallidie Plaza
Suite 250
San Francisco CA 94102
☎ (415) 981-5517

INDEX

Acknowledgements

The author wouls like to thank the staff at the German National Tourist Office in London and those in the regional and local resorts featured in this book, for their unstinting helpfulness and cooperation; also the staff of the rail, river and road transport undertakings — including the AA and ADAC motoring organisations — which have so helpfully provided information, illustrations or facilties.

He also acknowledges his gratitude to the Mittel-Mosel families whose friendship over many years stimulated and extended his acquaintance with the German wine-lands in the river valleys that are the subject of this book; in particular, the Melsheimer family of Siebenborn and the families of the late Georg Jahn of Bernkastel-Andel and of his friend the late Willi Willems of Brauneberg.

MPC

A Note to the Reader

Thank you for buying this book, we hope it has helped you to plan and enjoy your visit. We have worked hard to produce a guidebook which is as accurate as possible. With this in mind, any comments, suggestions or useful information you may have would be appreciated.

Please send your letters to:

The Editor
Moorland Publishing Co Ltd
Moor Farm Road West
Ashbourne
Derbyshire
DE6 1HD

The Travel Specialists

Visitor's Guides

Tour & Explore with MPC Visitor's Guides

Austria

Austria: Tyrol & Vorarlberg

Britain:

Cornwall & Isles of Scilly

Cotswolds

Devon

East Anglia

Guernsey, Alderney and Sark

Hampshire & Isle of Wight

Denmark

Jersey

Kent

Lake District

Scotland: Lowlands

Somerset, Dorset & Wiltshire

North Wales and Snowdonia

North York Moors, York & Coast

Northumbria

Northern Ireland

Peak District

Sussex

Yorkshire Dales & North Pennines

Crete

Cyprus

Egypt

Finland

Florida

France:

Alps & Jura

Corsica

Dordogne

Loire

Massif Central

Normandy Landing Beaches

Provence & Côte d'Azur

Germany:

Bavaria

Black Forest

Rhine & Mosel

Southern Germany

Iceland

Italy:

Florence & Tuscany

Italian Lakes

Northern Italy

Mauritius, Rodrigues & Reunion

Peru

Spain:

Costa Brava to Costa Blanca

Mallorca, Menorca, Ibiza & Formentera

Northern & Central Spain

Southern Spain & Costa del Sol

Sweden

Switzerland

Tenerife

Turkey

Yugoslavia: The Adriatic Coast

World Traveller

The new larger format Visitor's Guides

Belgium & Luxembourg

Czechoslovakia

France

Holland

Norway

Portugal

USA

MPC Guides
Explore the World with the Best in Travel Guides

Off the Beaten Track
Austria
Britain
France
Greece
Italy
Portugal
Scandinavia
Spain
Switzerland
West Germany

Spectrum Guides
African Wildlife Safaris
Kenya
Maldives
Pakistan
Seychelles
Tanzania
Zimbabwe

Insider's Guides
Australia
Bali
California
Eastern Canada
Western Canada
China
Florida
Hawaii
Hong Kong
India
Indonesia
Japan
Kenya
Malaysia & Singapore
Mexico
Nepal
New England
Spain
Thailand
Turkey
Russia

A complete catalogue of all our travel guides to over 125 destinations is available on request